I0528413

HOW TO LIVE
ANXIETY FREE

By Geoffrey A. Cole – A.R.M, CLC

BOOTSTRAP
PUBLICATIONS

Special discounts on bulk quantities of Bootstrap Publications books are available. For details contact:
Bootstrap Publications
Email: info@bootstrappublications.com

Library of Congress Cataloging in Publications Data
Cole, Geoffrey. (May 1963)
How to Live Anxiety Free / Geoffrey Cole
Paperback ISBN: 978-1-959220-09-1
Hardcover ISBN: 978-1-959220-08-4
© 2024 Geoffrey A. Cole

Printed in the United States of America on environmentally conscious material.

This book is dedicated to the love of my life, Jeanine, and my family, friends, and clients, without whom this book would not have been possible. I wish all of you and those that read this book an anxiety-free existence.

HOW TO LIVE ANXIETY FREE

By Geoffrey A. Cole – A.R.M, CLC

TABLE OF CONTENTS

FOREWORD 13

PREFACE..17

INTRODUCTION 33

WHAT IS ANXIETY..37

    Sources of Anxiety...40

    Panic Attacks vs. Anxiety Attacks....................................42

    The Difference between Anxiety and Depression.....................44

OVERCOMING TRAUMA 47

    Let Go of Guilt..49

    It Starts In The Womb..51

    Stress in the Body... 52

    Facing the Pain While Facing the Future............................ 57

    Using Sleep to Change... 59

THE "MIND MAP" 61

    Understanding Human Instincts And Nervous Systems 68

    Needs vs. Wants for Present Day 75

    The Cole Trapezoid..77

MENTAL WELLNESS TREATMENT ALTERNATIVES................. 87

    Category One – Mental Health issues.............................. 88

    Category Two – Cognitive Performance Improvement............. 88

    Category Three – Neurological Issues.............................. 88

    Category Four – Longevity...89

    Talk Therapy and Physical Therapy 89

    Treatment via Medications...90

    Meditation 91

    Yoga 92

Thai Chi and Qigong And Other Forms Of Martial Arts) 92

Plant Medicine 93

Religious, Spiritual, And Energy Healing Modalities 94

Neurofeedback 95

EMDR, Binaural Beats And Other Bidirectional Therapies 95

12-step Programs and Alcohol and Drug Rehabilitation Centers 96

Transcranial Magnetic Stimulation (TMS) And MeRT therapies 98

THE APPLICATION OF BIOFEEDBACK 101

Why Use Biofeedback Or Neurofeedback 105

Brainwave Feedback (Neurofeedback) And Controlling Stress 106

Retrain Your Muscles for Desired Functioning 108

Migraine Headache Prevention 110

Blood Pressure Measurement 111

Alpha Feedback And Pain Relief 111

Neurofeedforward 112

HOW NEUROEMPOWERMENT DIFFERS 117

Ask Yourself "What Do I Want?" 123

You Can Transform 124

You Are Not The Slave Of Your Nervous System 128

Our Tribal Instincts Rob Us Of Our "Power" 137

Finding Your Inner Peace and Personal Power 140

Self Betterment Exercises 144

What We Do at The Supermind Center 151

THE NEUROEMPOWERMENT PROCESS 160

Become Aware 161

Live Courageously 164

What Are Your Values Exercise 166

ENDNOTES 173

FOREWORD

As you will discover in the following pages, Geoff (aka G) Cole was briefly incarcerated. Simply by being himself, being present to the reality of the situation, and responding with the right attitude and mindset, he had quite an impact on his 50 or so cellmates. A short time after being released, he ran into one of them, who told him that there was still no fighting among them even a month after G's departure. In contrast, the neighboring cell remained quite violent. "You changed the consciousness of the cell," he told G.

That comment encapsulates this book, which guides and inspires the reader to "change the consciousness of the cell," both in the micro and macro senses. In these pages, Geoff shares much wisdom, including information about brain neuroplasticity, to help readers handle anxiety in their personal lives. In doing so, we can change not just our lives but our world.

Changing the consciousness of our cells is a concept that blends spirituality, alternative medicine, and holistic health practices. It suggests that our thoughts, emotions, and beliefs can influence the behavior and health of our cells. While this idea is not yet widely accepted in mainstream science, some alternative and complementary therapies explore the mind-body connection and its potential effects on cellular health.

I have been facilitating retreats and transformational coaching for over 30 years. The most effective healing tool I use is breathwork. The breath is at the core of every meditation technique and spiritual practice. It is also a remarkable gateway to understanding the intricate dance between neuroplasticity and mindfulness practices. Mindful breathing techniques, such as deep and focused breathing, have been found to induce profound changes in the brain's structure and function. These practices, often associated with meditation and yoga, can stimulate neuroplasticity by promoting the growth of new neural connections and enhancing the brain's adaptability. Regular, conscious control of the breath not only calms the mind but also triggers neuroplastic changes that can lead to increased attention, emotional regulation, and overall mental well-being. This intricate connection between the breath and neuroplasticity illustrates how something as fundamental as our breath can be a powerful tool for shaping and rewiring the brain, ultimately fostering a deeper understanding of the mind-body-spirit connection.

As Geoff points out, mindfulness is key to freeing ourselves from anxiety. Fear and anxiety tend to be future-based. Most often when we are anxious, we are scaring ourselves—consciously or not—about some future outcome that may—or may not—come to be. The present is the only thing we know is real and not a figment of our mind, whether a memory or a projection or hallucination about a possible future. Developing the skill to remain focused on the present takes intention and practice but it is something we can all learn. Remaining present—accepting the reality of his situation in the jail cell and drawing on his resources to deal with it—allowed G. to deal successfully with those extremely challenging conditions. Mindfulness practices enhance our self-awareness and provide the tools needed to be present.

Though Geoff's work is based on science, it is also spiritual. Which brings me back to the power of the breath. As I discuss in my TEDx talk by the same name, scientists haven't studied the effects on the brain when we breathe consciously in the same way they have meditation. One thing that helps me understand the profoundly healing and transformational effects of conscious breathing is the fact that in many spiritual traditions and even some secular languages, the same word can mean breath or spirit, depending on the context.

Spirituality and neuroplasticity also intersect in the realm of personal growth and healing. People who have faced trauma or challenging life experiences often find solace and resilience through spirituality. Neuroplasticity provides a scientific foundation for understanding how engaging in spiritual practices, such as mindfulness or forgiveness, can aid in the recovery process. These practices can lead to structural changes in the brain that help individuals cope with stress, anxiety, and emotional pain. In this way, neuroplasticity not only deepens our comprehension of spirituality but also underscores its practical benefits in promoting mental and emotional well-being, highlighting the profound synergy between the mind's adaptability and the journey of the spirit.

It is absolutely possible to live a life free from the grip of anxiety. Imagine waking up each morning with a sense of calm and confidence, ready to embrace the day's challenges. Picture yourself navigating life's twists and turns without the burden of constant worry. Living without anxiety means experiencing a profound sense of liberation, where your mind is free to explore the boundless possibilities of each moment. It's a heroic journey that involves self-discovery, resilience, and a commitment to your own well-being. With the right tools, support, and mindset, you can rewrite the narrative of your life, one filled with courage, peace, and the unwavering belief that you are in charge of your destiny. For you are the author of your story, not a character in someone else's. Your path to an anxiety-free existence begins with the decision to step forward, one fearless stride at a time. This book will help you get there.

*****

Christian de la Huerta is a transformational coach, TedX speaker, and award-winning author. For over 30 years he has supported clients to achieve their greatest potential by reclaiming their power, conquering insecurities, creating dream relationships, and living a life filled with fulfillment, meaning and purpose.

His newest book, *Awakening the Soul of Power*, inspires readers to discover new ways that transform their relationship to power, generating deeper levels of fulfillment and personal freedom. Music icon Gloria Estefan called it "a balm for the soul of anyone searching for truth and answers to life's difficult questions." It has received a Nautilus Book Award, Global Book Award, Book Excellence Award, and Nonfiction Book Award.

PREFACE

I felt a great deal of anxiety for most of my life. It impacted my ability to function and interrupted my work and relationships. Dealing with these high levels of anxiety ultimately brought about the crisis that led to my journey of finding relief. My perceptions and beliefs were absorbed from my upbringing, and even my parents' upbringing, which contributed to my pain and anxiety. Societal messages about controlling my emotions didn't help. The good news is that, as I struggled, I learned many valuable lessons which I then incorporated into my professional life. Now, I can support others in their journey to anxiety-free living.

At around 8 years old, I distinctly remember deciding I wanted to live my life trying to fit in with the people around me. I decided that I needed a lot of money so I could buy a lot of things. Unknowingly, I lived life in a way that trained my body to create stress and anxiety. I chased a hedonistic lifestyle as I became older and accumulated more things. I treated myself and my life as an amusement park; always looking for the next ride. "If you want to play, you have to pay," became my motto. I developed errant perceptions and understandings of the world that were not healthy or sustainable.

Around the age of 33, this lifestyle abruptly stopped working. I realized that I needed to make some changes, though I wasn't sure what they were. Spoiler alert: They turned out to be internal not external. The main things that I had to change were my belief systems which created and fueled my perceptions and behaviors. Since then, I have been on a journey of change — a journey that has led me to the complete and joy-filled life that I am living today.

My belief system at 33 revolved around the need for success, respect, money, possessions, and behaviors. At that time in my life, I believed feelings were for the weak. I did not trust emotions or have any use for them. In fact, I actually thought that emotions were bad. Since I believed that my happiness depended on things like success and possessions, I should have had everything to *make* me happy. I was a CEO, a homeowner, and a business owner. I bought high-end cars and other fancy things.

As I chased success and happiness, I also thought I had to negotiate for the upper hand in all situations. Of course, this meant that someone else was getting the lower hand. Losing. Economists since Adam Smith have told us that competition leads to economic success (if you win, of course). My understanding was that it is your duty to watch out for your own interests in a free-market society. So, if I "screwed" you, it was your fault. My way of thinking was horrible, and it led me down some dark paths. The consequences of this mindset eventually hit me hard. In 2001, on my 37th birthday, I was worth over $8,000,000. Within two months, I was destroyed and eventually was worth a negative $8,000,000.

What followed was mental, physical, emotional, philosophical, and spiritual anguish. I was accused of fraud, racketeering, and theft. Dealing with the fallout from my perception of the world brought me pain and anxiety. My heart would pound so hard and so rapidly that it was the only thing I could focus on.

I could not function during these moments. I thought I might die. In addition, my digestive system went completely haywire, and I had constant stomach pain and nausea. I couldn't sleep, couldn't focus, and I felt completely depressed to the extent that I sometimes couldn't even get out of bed. It was very hard to do anything, and I cried a lot. I felt like a total failure. I felt ashamed, angry, and frustrated with my circumstances, and I was so preoccupied that I was clumsy and felt completely consumed with how bad everything was. Because my fall was so fast and so hard, I couldn't find a way to hope for the future. It was a very difficult and negative time for me.

I had always been a church member. In a way, though, I treated my spiritual life as I did my business and personal life: I believed that if I showed up, prayed, and tithed appropriately, God would take care of me. When the proverbial excrement hit the proverbial fan, I felt as if all that I believed regarding God and his loving care had been incredibly wrong. At the same time, I started to believe that my downfall was (like Babylon) a message of punishment for my self-centered philosophy. My spiritual crisis added to the devastation I was feeling and experiencing in my life. I didn't know it at the time but came to understand that my mistakes and failures are valuable lessons. Instead of experiencing them as failures, I have incorporated the lessons learned into my philosophy and methods.

My belief that I was strong and could handle the world was pummeled down. I now felt utterly helpless and useless. I began to feel that it wasn't only my beliefs that were wrong, but that *I* was wrong. When everything was falling apart, I felt worthless. All the ways that I measured success were crumbling, and I eventually began to question whether I should exist. I suffered from codependency, and the person I was most dependent on at the time suggested that "a real man would do what it takes to get his life insurance to provide for his family when he cannot." I started to believe that I, and the people around me, were better off if I were dead. I started to think that I would cause less damage if I didn't exist. Having a life insurance policy made the idea that I was more valuable dead than alive even more real.

As the fallout continued to affect more of my life, my relationships with my wife and children deteriorated. I planned my suicide. While it truly seemed the best decision at the time, I was fortunate that friends and family helped me change my mind, which oddly made it even harder to live. Before, I had a way out. Now, I had to find a way to live through all the oppression. Things got much worse before they got better. I went through a very contentious divorce which made it difficult to have a normal relationship with my children. I felt that I was losing everything.

Scared and negative thoughts took over my existence.

"I cannot believe this is happening."

"I cannot stand this pain." "I feel stuck and do not know what to do."

"I feel extremely tired, and I do not have energy to live, let alone try to accomplish anything."

"I might as well just give up."

"I am worthless."

"I have tried so many things, and nothing seems to work for me,"

"I feel all alone with my problems."

"There is no one who can help me."

"God take me now. I do not have the will to live."

Just "showing up" became most of my battle. I began to live life without expectations, hopes, or dreams.

I had always had a very close relationship with my father. We worked together, and I relied on him as a support and adviser. I was devastated when he was diagnosed with Myelodysplastic Syndrome, a group of disorders caused when something disrupts the production of blood cells. He became very ill and was in and out of the hospital during this time. Our business began to fail. I found out later that my dad had done a number of questionable things out of desperation during his illness. In 2001 he passed away in my arms. I had to deal with the results of his desperate — but hurtful — actions and his death at the same time.

Following my dad's death and in the midst of a divorce, I became horribly, deeply depressed and emotionally drained. Anxiety and stress filled my days. There were a total of thirty-three lawsuits against me at the time, and my personal life was in shambles. I had neither time nor ability to feel much of anything, but, paradoxically, I cried much and often. I did very little to help myself feel better; I simply didn't have the knowledge of how my thoughts, feelings, and actions were connected. It's difficult to convey how awful I felt for months, even to the point of experiencing several terrifying breaks from reality. I felt like I was in hell.

The depth and magnitude of my stress and anxiety — and the toll they took on me — were extreme. I was sick for two weeks out of every month and developed severe back issues, headaches, and sciatica. It literally hurt me to breathe. Sleeping was nearly impossible. My ability to function dropped significantly, and my anxiety levels rose even higher, resulting in severe panic attacks and anxiety attacks. They're actually different things, which we'll talk about later.

In order to support my family, I waited tables at a Mexican restaurant and sold health insurance door to door. I judged myself heavily for my downfall, going from being CEO of six corporations worth millions of dollars to a waiter and door-to- door salesman. I gave my ex-wife the proceeds from selling our house and as much money as I could from my work. Surviving during this time was extremely difficult.

I began to realize that one of the factors that contributed to my distress was that I had a high level of limiting beliefs. I was trapped in a cycle of belief that things *shouldn't* be this way, that my life *shouldn't* be so hard. As the pressure on me built and my life and health worsened, I gradually had to shift my beliefs. I don't think I would have survived if I hadn't found a way to do this. At this time in my life, I perceived and judged all things as if they were "good" or "bad". Since it seemed so many bad things were happening, my continual judgment added to my anxiety and stress. My opinions were literally killing me slowly. My body was beginning to break down.

Finally, I began to try something new. I would detach from my opinion by saying to myself that my opinion "Doesn't F*cking Matter - DFM." When something happened around me, I would "DFM" the first thought (judgment) about it, take some deep breaths, and then search for the truth.

As time went on and I was able to adjust my perceptions, my life became less chaotic. My body began to feel a bit better. I was surprised when my depression and anxiety improved. With these small successes in place, I continued to search for more ways to alleviate my distress and improve my circumstances. People had a lot of ideas, and I read a lot of self-help books, but most of these things didn't work for me. Then someone told me to work on gratitude and acceptance. That turned out to be a key component of my healing.

I started making a "gratitude list" every day and worked on acceptance. It helped me move from a space of bargaining and ruminating over what had happened to accepting my situation (and understanding that it could be worse). But I was still miserable. I was in a deep, dark hole, and thinking about things differently could only take me so far. I began concentrating on my daily actions. I felt like I wanted to stay home in bed, so I got up and kept doing things instead. I could not think of my way into feeling better. I had to take good action so I could change my thoughts, and ultimately change how I felt.

In the spirit of "fake it 'til you make it," I decided to concentrate on creating more good energy than bad energy. Creating a gratitude list was not enough to create good energy. I learned that if I celebrated (with some physical movement) each item on the list, I then was creating lots of good energy. I still practice celebrating as a means of conditioning my nervous system to create joyous energy to this day. I actually throw my arms up and say (or shout) "Yes I am blessed" to celebrate everything I am grateful for.

Here is a sample Gratitude list:

I am grateful for,

- All of my talents

- My wife

- My car

- Food to eat

- My family and friends etc.

As I continued to confront my faulty perceptions, I came to understand that I could get help from people that understood how the brain worked and how to correct my flawed patterns of thinking. This was when I met the Reverend Dr. Francis Flynn (Skip). Dr. Flynn has a Psy.D. in clinical psychology and has specialized in family counseling for more than 20 years. In my first session with Skip, I discussed the problems I was having trying to save my marriage. He ended up being integral to my healing journey, even after divorce was inevitable and the best option for my continued healing.

I began calling Skip every day and meeting with him once a week. He helped me to understand that being human has many aspects, not just performing well and looking good. He helped me to realize that I had no idea what emotions were. I had been living a calculated life full of negotiations (known and unknown). Since all my thoughts were based on living out what I had calculated, I did not know how to feel anything beyond the very basic emotions: sad, angry, or happy.

Skip helped me identify where I felt my emotions in my body. Little by little, he helped me to understand that I should not be afraid of them. He liked to say "They are just emotions. They can't kill you." He taught me that they were a part of living. Some people say that they are the best part of living. Emotions are occurring whether I acknowledge them or not.

I began to see how bodily pain and discomfort were directly linked to certain emotions, and I was able to track how those emotions were affecting different parts of my body in different ways. For example, when I thought about my father's hurtful actions and death, I felt pressure around my heart and behind my eyes. When I felt that I was being disrespected, it felt as if the anger traveled from around my heart and the lower part of my neck into my shoulders, lower back, and face. The daily physical neural effect of these emotional charges was causing lasting pain in my body.

Skip referred me to a chiropractor, who introduced me to a process called Neuroemotional Technique (N.E.T.)[1], a chiropractic technique developed by Dr. Scott Walker to normalize unresolved physical, mental, and behavioral patterns in the body. This process helps release emotions from where they are trapped in the body. Trapped!

The concept of physically entrapped emotions fascinated me and propelled me to learn more and more. After two or three treatments, my pain went away. The emotions attached to those areas began to have less power. The things that were my emotional triggers — my divorce, my dad, my diminished circumstances — had been causing me extreme pain. Because I was not processing the emotions, they were ripping me apart.

After N.E.T., I was free from the trap that anxiety held me in. The neck, back, and sciatica pain went away. I was enjoying a new freedom. I began to ask myself what I asked many of my clients today who come to me for relief from their anxiety or panic attacks. "Is what you feel worth the imprisonment it causes?" I ask this because few people realize we can become prisoners to our thoughts and beliefs.

Two other tools helped me immensely during this period of negativity and darkness. I began to find peace through meditation and religious connection. The next year was filled with pain and agony as I transitioned from the life of a self-centered, success-driven "yuppie" into a love-centered person driven by helping others. Everything that I identified as a part of my sense of self-being was being ripped from my clutching fingers. I based my identity on what I owned, and it was ripped from me along with my possessions.

My career was my identity, not something I did for a living. Therefore, when I lost my job, that part of me was also lost in a way. I had to endure many identity deaths all at once: an involved father, a CEO, a friend, a husband, a son, etc., each of which was a terribly painful loss, both mentally and physically.

With the help of many, many tools and people, I slowly began to see that I had a very limited, perhaps demented, view of reality. I realized that I had to let go of everything that I thought defined me. I had to re-assess who I was. Up to that point in my life, I thought people who were not bent on becoming wealthy were not *real* men and women. They were almost lesser beings, or, at the very least, ignorant and misguided.

I had to change my frame of reference to valuing everything in my life. I gradually came to understand that the criteria I used to judge others was the same criteria I used to judge myself. I was causing myself pain by judging each moment instead of living in it. For the next eight years I had to learn how to look at and live my life differently. I would wake up in the depths of depression every day. My brain and body would tell me that there was no reason for me to get up because my life was not worth living, so I should just kill myself rather than struggle to get out of bed. Intellectually, I knew that was not true. Unfortunately, my default functioning had become suicidal, anxious, and depressive. So, every day I had to decide to take different actions to overcome my thoughts. This began my journey of internal awareness.

Skip taught me that we can feed the positive, or we can feed the negative. My new daily "job" became taking more positive actions than negative actions. On a typical morning, I would wake up feeling like I was in a deep, dark hole of hell. I would force myself to get out of bed and spend time meditating and taking care of the basics just so I could show up for my life and everybody in it.

On most days, I was successful in retiring at night as a relatively happy person. Unfortunately, while sleeping, the depression would return, and the next morning I'd have to go through the recovery process all over again. I began journaling during this time. I soon realized that having a written record of how I felt was invaluable. It is extremely hard to remember how I felt last week or last month. The written record kept track of that for me. My journaling showed me that I was taking all the right steps to living a happier life. Journaling helped me identify the role of my sleep patterns in contributing to my ongoing anxiety and depression. However, I was still waking up very depressed every day.

In 2002, I married Jeanine, who I think of as an angel sent from God. She really rescued me. She has been an important part of my life. She asked me what I wanted to do with my life, professionally. I told her I wanted to help others who were struggling like I had been. She and I decided that I would study psychology and dedicate my life to helping others. I also knew that I had to keep moving forward in my own personal development. I had come so far, but I knew that I still had very far to go.

In 2003, my wife (Jeanine) and I began opening "sober living" houses and hired Skip to be the psychologist in charge. I was paid to manage the houses. I began to study psychology and work under Skip as a counselor. During this time, I was still in constant legal battles with my ex-wife and in corporate litigations. Yet I was living a relatively happy life. I had learned to trust that all was okay and was going to be okay.

In January 2004, the corporate litigation finalized, resulting in a multimillion dollar judgment against me, increasing at 9% a year. I was still waking every day with a deep, dark depression which seemed to cause as much internal wreckage as a hurricane hitting the coast. I realized I had to focus on my sleep to get out of this vicious cycle that allowed me to only progress so far, having to refocus every single morning.

Unfortunately, the years of stress and anxiety took a toll. It exacerbated an arthritic condition, forcing me into a wheelchair. My physicians prescribed an opiate-based painkiller. I had a hip replacement. Like so many others, I ended up becoming dependent on opiates. Unless you've been hooked on opiates, it is impossible to describe how horrible the detoxification process makes you feel. Since I was already struggling with depression, opiate withdrawal pushed me further into that spiral. Every evening at sunset, my mood would drop with the setting sun, to near suicidal levels. I kept getting waves of anxiety and panic, coupled with that deep, dark feeling of utter despair and depression.

I applied the tools I'd been learning to this new period of anxiety and depression, leaned heavily on my wife (Jeanine), and managed to regain some equilibrium, but a second hip replacement in 2007 brought all those feelings back with full force. I was so fortunate at this juncture to have Jeanine in my life and to hear about a new technology called Brainwave Optimization, invented by a group of scientists in Arizona. Adding this treatment to my regimen was miraculous, and I began to study with the inventors so I could help others use this modality.

Around 2010, as a way to support my children through the changes resulting from my divorce, I had multiple interactions with psychologists. I found something surprising: Most psychologists don't track any empirical data on how well their methods actually help patients. I felt very disheartened during this time that I wouldn't have any way of knowing who'd be able to help my children.

In addition, I received no help from the Family Court system or the mental health system, (both of these probably need reform, but that's for another book) and that was extremely difficult and frustrating for me as a father. Ultimately, my confrontations with these systems devastated my family. My daughter ran away repeatedly, which was heartbreaking, and I was unfairly jailed for 60 days in 2013.

It was a very difficult time, but, I have to say, I learned a lot during my stay in jail, and those lessons continue to aid me on my own journey of recovery and in how I help others. It also showed me how I can have a broader impact in the world through NeuroEmpowerment.

I was in a situation unlike any I had ever experienced before. I was able to use the tools I'd been developing even in this situation of extreme duress. One of these tools I use to help me maintain my happiness is "the sweet delicious breath" (I explain this in more detail later in the book). This is one of the tools I developed to heal my depression, and I continue to use it on a daily basis. While I was in jail, my fellow inmates kept asking me "What is wrong with you? We are in jail, and you are happy." I can feel happy in good times and bad, partially because of my "sweet delicious breath".

Another great experience was changing the consciousness of the cell. The cell I was placed in was one of two cells near downtown Miami that are attached to a courtroom. Each cell houses 50 to 60 men. In a jail cell, as it is in many tribal situations, the newcomers are usually scared (possibly with good reason) so they start a fight in order to "get respect" which often will help them be safer. On my fourth day in the cell, a newcomer picked me to fight with. He said, "I don't like your face. I am gonna kick your ass".

I responded with, "What are you scared of?"

He said, "I ain't scared of nothin', I'm gonna kick your ass!"

I said very loudly, "You are scared of getting stabbed" I then looked around the room and said loudly, "Is anybody going to stab this guy today?"

Everybody in the cell started laughing...

I turned to the guy and said, "We all have to do some time here. Let's try to make the best of it."

In my efforts to "make the best of it", I helped create sudoku classes, bible studies, meditation training, group work-out sessions, chess tournaments, and "casino nights" in our cell. This definitely had an influence on our cell.

The fighting in my cell stopped. In the cell next to mine, the fighting continued as it always did. I was in that cell for 30 days. I was then moved to a trustee cell. When I was released, on my way out, I was handcuffed to a guy who looked at me and said, "I remember you. You are that guy that changed the consciousness of the cell."

I questioned, "What do you mean?"

He said, "The fighting in our cell has stayed stopped for the last 30 days when you were not there anymore. You changed the consciousness of the cell."

I was one of 50-60 guys who came in and out of the cell every three days. If you do the math, I was basically 1 of 1000 men who came through that cell whose consciousness changed. This was my direct experience with the 1/1000th principle of changing a population. I am following this formula in my quest to help the world become a love-based place. I only have to help 7 million people for that to happen.

That's powerful knowledge! Jail is rough. I observed and experienced many of the foundations of what causes so much trouble and hardship in the lives of mankind. I had the opportunity to directly study, and experience how our animal instincts can govern our behaviors, and I saw firsthand what generations of oppression can do.

I learned that what we do or say has a significant impact on the consciousness of ourselves and others. That lesson was solidified during my stay in jail and has since been a part of my life. It is also one of the reasons I am writing this book. I used these tools during the worst period of my life to positively impact mine and my cell mates' experiences. It was nothing less than magical.

I will be forever grateful that while I was in jail I got a crash course on how the world I lived in outside was not the same world that many of the men that I was incarcerated with lived in. I was provided with insight I couldn't have received had I not been incarcerated. Even with the hardships — death, business failures, divorce — that I was living through, I still had advantages in education and life circumstances. Not to mention I never faced the oppression and racism that many of these men had. Our perspectives were so different, each based on our own life circumstances. But here we were forced together in the same place, and I had some things to learn.

As I spent more time with them, I began to see that we struggled with the same issues. Our various hardships and the things we were each taught about the world had affected our judgment, our ability to be vulnerable, our sense of self-worth, and our beliefs about what it takes to be safe, survive, and thrive. I wanted to feel better. I wanted to feel worthy of having a better life with less hardship and more joy, less pain and more energy. As we had conversations and were able to share some of these things with each other, I was given opportunities to learn and opportunities to share the things I'd been learning that were helping me recover my own life. Sharing these tools in incarcerated and newly released populations remains some of the most gratifying and important work that I'm engaged in.

I had to learn that I was more than my mistakes and failures, and as I learned that about myself and utilized the tools that I'd been developing to save my own life, I believe I was able to help my cellmates as well. All of us were suffering from believing the messages of "I am less than," "I am not good enough", "I am not worthy," and that success is dependent on what we have rather than who we are.

One of the most inspiring people that I met in jail was named Terril "Wolf" Lomax, may he rest in peace. He allowed me to share some tools and techniques with him, and his transformation was no less miraculous than my own. I went from an angry, broken man, whose life was in shambles in every area to a peaceful, loving presence for myself and my family. Likewise, Wolf went from being extremely angry and absent from his family — incarcerated for 19 of his 40 years when we met — to someone joyful, responsible, and successful.

From 2014 until he passed in 2022, he lived as a law-abiding member of society, employed, a good father, a good son, a good brother, and a good friend. As I learned to overcome what I was going through, he learned alongside me. Together, we learned how to get through stressful situations and keep moving forward. Although my incarceration was my rock bottom, I am grateful for my time there. That experience allowed me to test my methods in the worst possible circumstances. The experience contributed to the work I do helping the population become happier, calmer, successful, and more self-assured.

One of the final pieces to my process of healing was meditation. However, when I first began trying to meditate, I failed. My regrets, remorse, and resentment about my father dying, my wife leaving me, the lawsuits, the struggles of my children, and the loss of my assets and businesses, would not let me sit still long enough or self-direct my thinking or my feelings.

After I practiced for a while, I achieved a second or two of peace. I expanded that second or two into five or ten seconds. My ability to create peace in my mind kept expanding until I could do hours. My journey took me years, but it was all worth it.

I was able to fully test my new understandings and tools for better living through my mental wellness centers through which I have been helping others to achieve Anxiety Free Lives as well as help them with many other mental health issues and sometimes just help them perform and live their lives from a higher frequency (brain wave frequency)! As for the writing of this book, the center is Supermind Center, LLC. It is in the center where I have cemented and furthered my understanding and methods. I do not believe these methods are the "end all - be all" for living anxiety free, however, these methods have helped thousands of people improve their lives. There are other methods (some of which I discuss in this book) and even though a very high percentage of people do, not everyone gets everything they want from my methods. What is presented in this book is about ⅓ of the NeuroEmpowerment process. It has been very helpful for many people. In the center, through the complete process of NeuroEmpowerment, we are able to help with many other issues and take anxiety free living to higher levels for people who want more help. As stated in the foreword, at the center, we help people accomplish in days what can take a lifetime to achieve.

All the tools I learned that kept me alive during extremely difficult times are woven into my methods and in this book. I get to help people overcome hardship every day, using sessions of NeuroEmpowerment, which incorporates coaching, biofeedback, meditation, psychology, and a number of other tools into a cohesive system. I'm so excited to finally have something — this book — that I can share with even more people. I hope it helps you find the peace, success, and happiness that you deserve.

INTRODUCTION

This book is intended to provide a clear-cut explanation of how the nervous system functions and provides instructions on how to harness the power of neuroplasticity. Neuroplasticity, known as the neural plasticity (or brain plasticity) is the ability of neural networks[2] in the brain and the body to change through growth and reorganization. These changes range from individual neurons[3] making new connections to systemic adjustments like cortical remapping[4]. Neuroplasticity is the nervous system's mechanism for responding to changes in the environment, whether that is trauma or injury, changing a habit, or learning new information or behavior.

Advancements in technology and our sociological development have created a mad world. Studies show that the average person is processing more than 175 times more information on a daily basis than they did 100 years ago. However, reading and processing speeds have not increased enough to keep up. This disparity causes the majority of today's most challenging issues: anxiety, stress, depression, ADD/ADHD, addictions, sleep issues, and many more.

Once you understand this, it's easier to see how anxiety is created in the "self" and take steps to learn how to live "anxiety free." It is possible to reduce our levels of anxiety to a minimum in order to create and maintain "Anxiety-Free Living". After exhaustive probing, experimenting on my own healing, and delving into the minds and brains of many other anxious people, I am finally able to provide a process based on using neuroplasticity to achieve an anxiety free life.

According to Erik Erikson's stages of psychological development, between the ages of 6 to 11, it is natural for us to ask the question "How can I be good?." This question, however it shows up in the mind of the child, is the beginning of how we develop our inner picture of what it means to thrive. We basically create a formula of how we will live in order to be okay.

As we grow, we subconsciously create a life that aligns with that formula. If the initial process is flawed because of trauma or upheaval, it can be difficult to identify why we don't feel fulfilled or why we feel anxious or depressed. Sometimes, everything can look successful from the outside, but we struggle with thoughts like "there has to be more" or "something is missing". Harnessing the brain's powers of neuroplasticity can alleviate that stress, help us identify underlying anxiety or depression, and provide the basis for true and lasting change, fulfillment, and happiness.

This book gives you the ability to be the person you are meant to be. You will become aware of who you truly are and how to become the you that is filled with confidence, self-love, respect, and acceptance. Becoming the person you are meant to be is a step-by-step process of learning to trust yourself every day with renewed energy. You will unlock yourself from all the stress that has interfered with your goals and desires.

Are you ready for a real transformation? Have you had enough of the way things are? Do you feel trapped? How do you know when you are ready to change? The answer is, when you have had enough of the way things are! That is how you know it is time.

WHAT IS ANXIETY

Anxiety can be defined as any unwanted increase in nervous system energy. Anxiety manifests differently in each person but can feel like racing thoughts, nausea, increased heartbeat, thinking about "what ifs", ruminating about the same subject over and over again, sweating or cold sweats, panic attacks, talking continuously, not talking, having to DO something, or not wanting to do anything.

Many high performers are not even aware of their anxiety, yet it still exists in their unconscious. Unconscious anxiety typically manifests in physical ailments. Anxiety often manifests consciously when we become aware of a disconnect between how we believe life "should" be versus how it is.

You might remember from my personal story that I began to experience my life-changing, personal crisis when I was 33. My belief system at that time in my life was that I needed to have many things to be happy, things like success, respect, and money. My way of thinking was horrible, and it led me down some pretty horrible paths. I was 37 years old and worth more than $8,000,000. Within two months, I was destroyed and crippled by anxiety and depression. I learned many valuable lessons through this crisis which I then incorporated into my professional life. I now work in the amazing field of helping others take their journeys to living anxiety free.

While I hope that none of you reading this book have to experience the depths of despair and the multiple crises that I went through, I want you to know that if you're experiencing any of these symptoms, NeuroEmpowerment can help guide you to a better place. Especially if you identify with any of the following.

- bouts of nausea that come and go too often
- mental, physical, emotional, philosophical, or spiritual anguish
- rapid, pounding heart rate
- digestive system upsets including frequent diarrhea or constipation
- difficulty sleeping
- finding it difficult to show up and function at anything
- difficulty getting out of bed
- feeling depressed, sad, or crying a lot
- having a hard time focusing
- experiencing physical impacts (ex: increased clumsiness)
- experiencing high levels or frequent anger and frustration
- feeling hopeless, useless, trapped or at a dead end
- bouts of extreme nervousness
- believing suicide might be an option
- feelings of being punished by life or by God
- frequent feelings of shame, guilt, or remorse
- belief that you're a failure

If you are experiencing anything from the list above, you are a good candidate for using NeuroEmpowerment to take better control of your life. Read on to learn more about the brain-body connection and neuroplasticity or skip around to chapters calling you. How you use this book is up to you. You are in charge of your own healing process!

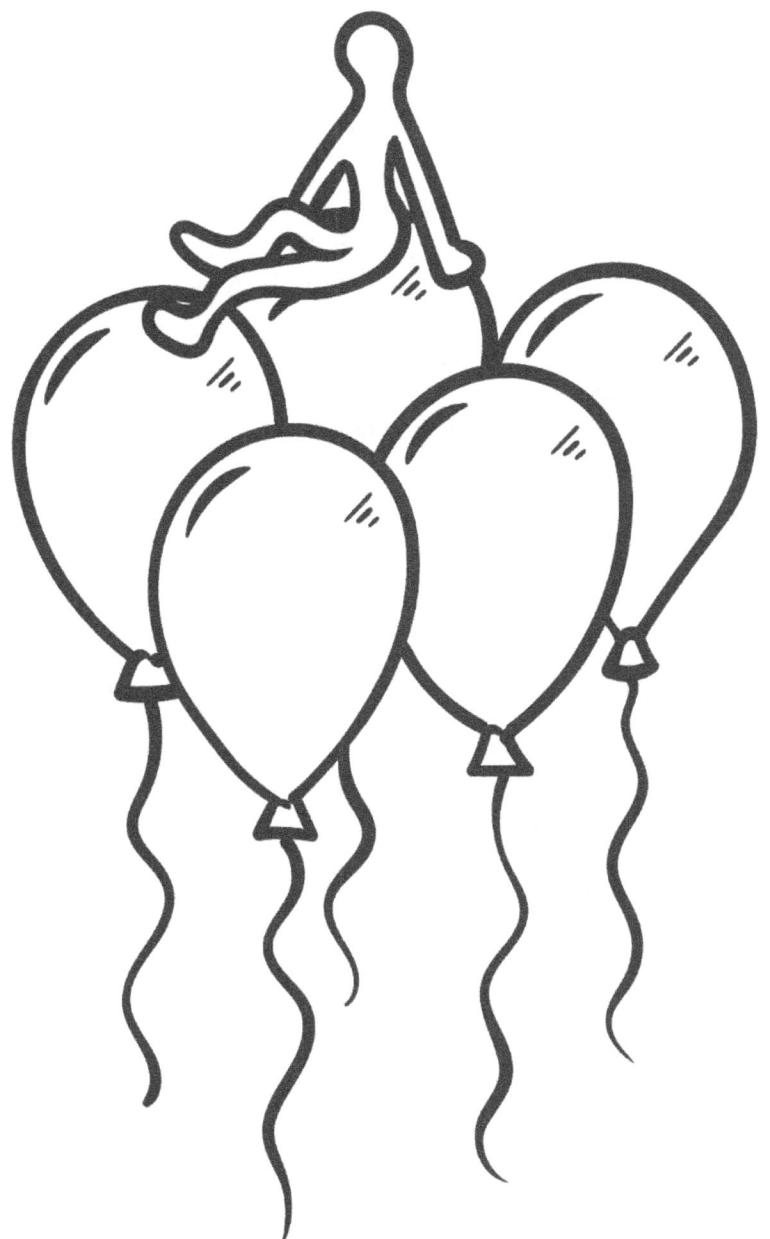

Live Anxiety Free

Sources of Anxiety

"That which does not kill us makes us stronger."
-Friedrich Nietzsche

"There are no mistakes, no coincidences. All events are blessings given to us to learn from."
-Elisabeth Kubler-Ross

Throughout this book, you will learn steps toward acceptance. True acceptance means that we understand that "it is what it is" without an opinion if it is good or bad. Acceptance of what is happening helps reduce anxiety and sadness. I found this to be true when I learned to apply acceptance to my life. Acceptance gave me the space to learn from my experiences. Loss always involves the grieving process. And grieving must occur before any learning can take place. I agree with Elisabeth Kubler-Ross, who stated that the stages of grieving are:

- Shock and Denial
- Frustration and Anger
- Bargaining
- Depression
- Acceptance

During the time period when scared and negative thoughts took over my existence, I had continual thoughts.

I cannot believe this is happening.
I cannot stand this pain.
I feel stuck and do not know what to do.
I feel extremely tired, and I do not have energy to live, let alone try to accomplish anything.
I might as well just give up.
I am worthless.
I have tried so many things, and nothing seems to work for me,"
I feel all alone with my problems. There is no one who can help me.
God take me now — I do not have the will to live.

I kept visiting the stages of grief mentioned above over and over again. While this is common when dealing with grief, it was very painful and frustrating until I found acceptance. When I accepted what was happening, I found the energy to try and create more positive energy than bad energy.

As you heard in my personal story, before I found acceptance, my anxiety level went over the top, including panic attacks so severely I would have trouble breathing. My nervous system had more control over my anxiety and panic than my conscious or intellectual parts of my nervous system.

Our brains and bodies are the source of anxiety. While not completely understood, the emotion of anxiety causes physical reactions. In addition, not only does anxiety manifest through the body and into our thoughts, but it also affects brain chemistry. Even future thoughts can be affected. Our past thoughts and experiences are housed in our subconscious and unconscious, as well as consciously. All of this is happening in our bodies.

Accordingly, the way we think about and perceive our lives directly affects the way our entire body operates. This dynamic also applies to your future thoughts. This is why I often say, "Pay attention to the thoughts you validate because they are becoming a part of you in your body."

Anxiety may develop with years of experiences piled on top of each other, creating habitual ways of perceiving and reacting. Interrupting these cycles, with the goal of calmness and acceptance, can be supported through biofeedback and mindfulness techniques.

These techniques are effective whether your own life experiences are causing you anxiety or if you're experiencing the effects of epigenetics (trauma handed down from generation to generation). Reframing our past, learning relaxation, cultivating acceptance, and changing behavior patterns can often stop anxiety as it begins and even prevent it from recurring.

The science of the brain and body shows that your nervous system functions by utilizing neurotransmitters. So, what are neurotransmitters? They consist of small chemicals inside your body and brain. They are typically used for messages from the brain to other parts of the nervous system or to muscles that send messages about how to feel, think, and act. These chemicals have names such as serotonin, GABA and norepinephrine. A common reason people experience anxiety symptoms is an excess of or a lack of serotonin. These chemicals can become unbalanced due to the way you live your life or because of genetic or health issues.

Many researchers believe that there are two different parts to an anxiety disorder, and a person with anxiety may suffer from one or both. One part is mental (worries, nervous thoughts, fear, and low self-esteem). The second part of anxiety is physical, like a racing heartbeat, panic attacks, lightheadedness, and feeling jittery. From my experience and research, I believe that anxiety disorders are always both. This reflects my perspective that we humans are both mind and body.

Many who have anxiety, especially those who've suffered for quite some time, often feel hopeless, as though their anxiety cannot be stopped or treated. Here is the good news: The brain and body are incredibly adaptive. They can respond to learning, experiences, and mental abilities. Through learning relaxation tools and coping mechanisms, we can reduce, eliminate, and control anxiety.

Panic Attacks vs. Anxiety Attacks

While some may use the terms "panic attack" and "anxiety attack" interchangeably, there is a difference. An easy way to remember the difference is that an anxiety attack can usually be traced to some cause in the environment, and it can last for hours. A panic attack comes suddenly, often without a traceable reason, and typically lasts only a few minutes. There are other differences, of course, but this may help you gain a working understanding of what you or someone in your life is experiencing.

Panic attacks are a particularly distressing form of anxiety. Researchers have found that those with panic attacks often have overactive amygdala. The amygdala is the part of the brain that determines threats in our environment and governs feelings of fear. Past research has shown that panic attacks cannot and will not be controlled while they are happening by using forceful methods. However, learned relaxation or meditation practiced over a period of time can prevent panic attacks or control them should they continue.

There are ways of using the power of neuroplasticity that can change the brain and body pathways that are associated with panic attacks. This can be accomplished more quickly with biofeedback and neurofeedback. Once learned and practiced, existing thinking and behaviors that are no longer useful can be changed, and by rewiring pathways to function in new and better ways they can be forged and made durable. What we practice becomes permanent (or at least long-lasting).

Anxiety attacks are usually, although not always, caused by severe stressors. Chronic anxiety is one of the most common mental health problems in the world and can be very hard to cope with. Most types of anxiety can also be managed over time with practice.

Memories of past events are often the cause of an onslaught of anxiety. In its most extreme form, this type of anxiety is called PTSD (Post Traumatic Stress Disorder). A good example is when veterans remember or re-live stressful scenes of what they witnessed in battle and don't know how to relieve themselves from those harrowing thoughts. Even events that seemed manageable at the time can, when remembered, bring up feelings of anxiety.

Other forms of anxiety include fear of public speaking, fear of heights, and other phobias, which can also trigger a racing heart rate and an inability to perform or complete designated tasks. Severe worry that something is or will go wrong can push us to an emotional breaking point. In the long run, it is more important to learn how to stop creating these fears than it is to just learn to cope with the anxiety they bring.

Rapid thinking, waves of fear, trouble making decisions and other forms of anxiety can interrupt an already busy day. This is especially true for those who are already stressed from multi-tasking and may be running on empty.

The Difference between Anxiety and Depression

It would be great if there were a fool-proof way of telling whether you have anxiety or depression. They are often intertwined. People can have both. In fact, some may have developed depression symptoms as a result of their anxiety disorder and vice versa. Both may have similar causes and result in the same issues in your life. They have different neurological indicators, and now neural assessments can provide a numerical scoring of the levels of anxiety and depression.

I have come to describe anxiety as your nervous system and belief systems interfering with you living as your most confident self. Anxiety always causes an increase in energy. A great way to resolve the symptoms caused by anxiety is to learn how to self-soothe or apply techniques which influence our nervous system to calm down. I will discuss this in more detail later in this book.

Depression, on the other hand, is an overall sense of sadness about the past, present, and/or future. It often comes with a feeling that everything is hopeless. Depression often causes a decrease in energy. I have often described my depression as a deep, dark hole filled with despair where hope does not exist. Depression can occur after experiences of anxiety, especially as the adrenaline produced by an anxiety attack disperses. An anxious person can end up feeling drained and hopeless. You might sleep too much or struggle with insomnia.

Both anxiety and depression can be relieved with mindfulness techniques and a process of rewiring brain activities. Training, practice, and awareness can reverse anxiety and depression. Learning mindfulness techniques and cultivating self-compassion are key to increasing our willingness to discover and recover ourselves. It's a two-way street, meaning that what has been "wired" into us can be unwired. Even if the pains of anxiety, depression, or both have caused days or even months of anguish, they can be eliminated, making life much more enjoyable.

Key Takeaways

Definition of Anxiety:
- Anxiety is any unwanted increase in nervous system energy, leading to symptoms like racing thoughts and rapid heartbeat. It can be conscious or unconscious, often rooted in early life experiences.

Impact of Unconscious Anxiety:
- Unconscious anxiety can cause physical ailments due to a disconnect between beliefs and reality. Early traumas can lead to flawed coping mechanisms, resulting in unfulfillment even in successful individuals.

Neuroplasticity and Healing:
- Understanding neuroplasticity helps identify underlying anxiety and/or depression and many other issues. NeuroEmpowerment fosters confidence and self-love, enabling transformation through harnessing neuroplasticity, and reorganizing neural connections, to promote healing.

Recognizing Anxiety:
- Symptoms include self-doubt, rapid heartbeat, high volumes of involuntary thoughts, and insomnia. Acceptance, reframing past experiences, changing perspectives, and relaxation techniques are essential for reducing anxiety.

Understanding Panic Attacks:
- Distinguish panic attacks from anxiety attacks; panic attacks are sudden and intense physical symptomologies, linked to an overactive amygdala. Neuroplasticity techniques like biofeedback and mindfulness can control panic attacks.

Anxiety vs. Depression:
- Anxiety involves heightened nervous activity, leading to agitation and stress, while depression brings sadness and decreased energy. Both can be managed through mindfulness and self-compassion practices.
- Learning mindfulness techniques and cultivating self-compassion can help eliminate anxiety.

OVERCOMING TRAUMA

Let's get on the same page on what trauma is as it relates to NeuroEmpowerment. Trauma comes in various forms and definitions. For NeuroEmpowerment, trauma is anything that impacts how our nervous system functions gained from our past which are no longer valid today. This includes anything from our past (experiences, genetics, and epigenetics) that causes errant beliefs and anxiety from our past. This could be beliefs or practices that are handed down generation to generation in our family or environment. Trauma can also be abusive or oppressive situations that we live through. Traumas very often shape our nervous system's understanding of reality making it difficult to recover from them.

The key is mindset. I have heard it said that "suffering is optional." I feel that this is a very insensitive statement. Suffering is often involuntary. In order to stop suffering, most of the time a mindset shift and reconditioning of the unconscious is necessary. This involves shifting beliefs, perspectives, and function. Making these kinds of shifts is often not possible, especially without help from others. A part of this is not merely being in the presence of others, it is being truly heard, seen, accepted, and appreciated by the people around us. We need to feel that we are held in someone else's mind and heart. For our physiology to calm down, heal and grow, we need a feeling of safety.

Most people who have had a history of trauma feel isolated and may have less trust in groups of people until they can be heard, listened to, and feel understood (even accepted). Another part of this is shifting our perspective of the traumas from traumatic events which harmed us or caused us loss, to valuable lessons and/or catalysts to live life differently. It often helps people to change their perspective when they have lost loved ones (or witnessed the loss) to the way they would want you to live from now on. It is not healthy to make this shift without going through the grieving process (I will discuss this later in the book). It is important to focus on and provide what each layer of the psyche needs in order to process, accept, and transition from trauma.

In an effort to keep us safe from trauma, our involuntary nervous system may cause us to relive our traumas over and over again which often gives us the feeling that it will last forever. This dynamic often manifests as circular thinking or persistent rumination. Often, following our animal instinctual desire to define everything and put it into "boxes", we review the particulars of the trauma and demand to know exactly what happened and how it happened. It is important for us to move from being the victims of trauma or loss to being the director of how to process, heal, and live in the now with acceptance and gratitude.

Therapy and/or meditation focused on processing and reconciling the past and living in the "present moment" can go a long way in helping people recover from trauma and thrive. The process usually includes some form of grieving, accepting, forgiving, and healing. Remember that our nervous system keeps track of everything in order to keep us safe (including traumas that happened).

Being anchored in the present while realizing that the trauma is not happening now may not ever happen again, and, at this point, happened only in the past, opens the ability for our nervous system to stop causing us to relive or think about the trauma. In the brain and body, it is natural to retain the neural pathways which cause us to relive past traumas which often leads to pain, depression, and anxiety. We want to train ourselves (mind, brain, and body) to let the past stay in the past.

Reactions to prior trauma can have a major impact on the present. Therapy, life coaching, biofeedback, and neurofeedback can help people experiencing trauma become aware of their feelings and see them from a different perspective. NeuroEmpowerment integrates all of these. That means feedback from therapists and technology can identify and alert patients to stress responses (and the precursor biological shifts) that may have been ignored in the past. Many operate in denial, frustrations, or even depression without being aware of what is going on in their minds and bodies. I have seen many people who just keep on moving. They basically try to keep running so they can run away from their problems. They may even keep thoughts and feelings to themselves because of shame, vulnerability, or simply being overwhelmed.

Reactions can be irrational and outside of one's control. Urges and emotions make people feel crazy, but quite often, they are not crazy, but unaware. Once one can observe themselves on a biofeedback machine, they can see their rapid heartbeat or their blood pressure rising. Observing this and getting a different perspective can go far in the realization and understanding of how the mind and body work together.

This realization of past and present trauma dynamics helps people truly embody their neuroplasticity and the ability to control and/or manage their trauma, anxiety or depression. Through NeuroEmpowerment, people can take this step further and stop or prevent their nervous system from creating trauma related energy. Oh, what a relief this can be.

Let Go of Guilt

Let's face it, when you didn't live up to your standards in the past, you violated yourself. You didn't even know it because you weren't as aware as you are now. You are no longer on that automatic pilot of the past. You were doing the best you could. You just didn't know any better. Accept that truth and forgive yourself. The point is, now you know how to treat yourself better. Let's give up the regrets, the weight of past suffering, and the guilt of the past. It is a new day, you have a new freedom to wipe the slate clean.

If a child lives with shame, he or she learns to feel ashamed. Some of you know that shame can drive anyone into obsessive control and perfectionism. Yelling, name calling, labeling, criticizing, judging, ridiculing, humiliation and comparing are all sources of shame driven by many forms of fear. For example, when one is taught that anger is sin, one becomes ashamed when he or she is angry. Substances can cover up the feeling of being "bad". And so, it is no surprise that an adult criticized or put down for some activity will relate to being criticized in the past. Running for the quick fix, whether food, behaviors, alcohol, or drugs, instant gratification is the possibility to dull the emotional pain.

The mistakes you made in the past do not mean you are a bad person. You were on the path to who you are now, and the beauty of your awareness now is that you can change. Your ability to change is even better now that you are willing and more able to make change and be inspired to continue to take steps toward your goals. Your reflection on and use of the past will continue to change. All of your regrets can become important assets for you to draw from in the future in order to help others.

You don't have to be continually punished for your past. Just knowing that allows the shame and blame to be a faint memory. You can let your guard down. After all, what are you afraid of? Strike that, be afraid of nothing. You are safe after all. You are not a child. Whatever is to come, you can handle.

Remember, when you consider what you are afraid of, you are actually creating synapses in your body to process that fear. You are literally creating the image of the fear in your body. The nerves which embody those fears will affect any future events which your nervous system believes are associated in any way. That is why I like to spend most of my time creating nerves focused on positive outcomes that are void of those fears. I work hard to not create the fear that blocks me anymore. More significantly, I work hard on creating positive energy (love and "I am safe") which is void of my fears, and I use that to counteract my fears.

It Starts In The Womb

The beginning and development of neural pathways which leads to how we feel and function on a daily basis begins in the last trimester of the pregnancy before we are born. As discussed previously, we are both mind and body. Let's briefly discuss the history of what is making us function the way we do today.

I have reviewed neural pathway mappings produced by electroencephalography (EEGs) from the scalp correlated with psychosocial histories taken from thousands of people. My findings are that tracking the cause of these issues is quite simple. Based on the development of neural pathways in the brain during pregnancy (in utero development) - sensory-motor neuron development occurs in the Occipital Lobe. This is, of course, patterned from our genetics and our environment which is directly related to the status of the mother and her environment.

The original sensory-motor patterns are created at that time. The original patterns then become a guide for the creation of all subsequent neurons and neural pathways (Neurogenesis and the other parts of Neuroplasticity). These are our original frame of reference for us to create all future neural pathways. Accordingly, our neurogenesis is directly driven by these original perceptions and understandings for the rest of our lives (at Supermind, we found that we can change these perceptions and understandings which can then change the patterning of our neurogenesis).[5]

Stress in the Body

When our body releases hormones, it activates our nervous system. Then, the adrenal glands trigger the release of adrenaline. This causes an increase in heart rate, blood pressure and breathing rate. After the stress is gone, it takes between 20 and 60 minutes (these times can be and often are less based on our past and our states of mind) for the body to return to a normal state.

You can probably think of a time when you experienced this fight or flight response. Your heartbeat quickened and you began breathing faster, and your entire body was able to run very fast. Even encountering a growling dog during your run, or as a result of a more psychological threat such as taking a test in school or giving a big presentation at work. Your heart beats faster in order to add oxygen as fuel as a rapid response to the danger. Your hands may become cold as the blood is rushing to your major organs. Your pupils dilate so that you become more aware of escaping the danger. It is also important to note that the response can be triggered due to both real and imaginary threats.

Stress can be helpful when it prompts you to perform better in situations where you are under pressure to do well, such as at work or school. Understanding the body's natural fight or flight response is one way to help you cope with stressful situations. When you understand these triggers and are triggered, you can start looking for ways to calm down and relax your body. It can be such helpful learning that your feeling of being out of control or overwhelmed can actually be an alert for you to understand and create a path back to normal calm. Everything described here regarding fight and flight is directly affected by our perceptions and states of mind. Mindfulness techniques can alter these states of mind and function.

Our bodies are equipped with a survival system which we entrain to function better or worse based on how we live our lives. An example of this system was discovered through a study of the hunters and gatherers of many years ago and the present behavior that flows through mind and body instantly when threatened. The hunters go out into the land to find food. Suddenly an angry, hungry animal appears! Their reaction as to whether they should stand their ground and fight or immediately turn and run is called the "fight or flight" response. This response automatically sends blood from the extremities to the heart and head to provide extra strength to the major organs. Adrenaline, at the same time, is released to provide power to run from the animal or to fight the animal and kill it before one is killed.

Another example is when an automobile cuts in front of you, you become instantly startled. Your body is instantly equipped as in the last example to react and slam on the brakes or pull around the car that has cut you off and caused you stress. How you react to the adrenaline rush may be with anger and rage or with relief for avoiding an accident. Whether you are angry or relieved is directly dependent on your state of mind, your experience, and/or your beliefs. All of this can be changed. This also directly affects if or how long it takes for your breathing to be restored and for you to return to feeling you are managing the situation and knowing that you are safe.

Research dating as far back as the 1960s, as stated in the book written by Boss M., "A Psychiatrist Discovers India[6]", showed that those who have had major stress in their lives can learn the steps to manage themselves from the inside after understanding what is really happening in their brains and bodies. Old beliefs that no longer serve us can be changed to help manage fear, loss, depression and anxiety. Neurofeedback can be used to help understand, measure, speed up, and strengthen this process. At Supermind we have performed tens of thousands of sessions of Neurofeedback on our clients and have seen miraculous results.

Some indicators that stress and anxiety are impacting you include:

- Waking up with no energy to get to work.
- Looking at your phone and getting distracted with the news or social media.

- Allowing a message that comes from someone to interrupt what you are doing because "you need to answer right away"; forgetting what is really important to yourself on this day.
- Do all the things that didn't get done yesterday.
- Worry about work comes to mind or stays embedded deeply in our psyche and bodies.
- A feeling of overwhelm..." I can't do this", "I am not good enough", "I can't do it all."
- Also, every family has needs... "Gotta pick up the kids, my aging parents need me today." Feeling stuck in the middle of it all.
- "Do more, do more, do more" comes into the mind.

As multi-taskers thinking "do more do more do more" could be a conscious belief or embedded deeply in our subconscious and unconscious, either way, our involuntary nervous system takes this as a serious threat to our survival. For some, the feeling of being overwhelmed rises every day. These parts of ourselves are not just feelings but distinct parts of our "survival being". These learned roles and agendas are usually ever mounting.

What is the answer? It begins with Emotional Intelligence[7]. Listening to, identifying the voices you can trust, and discarding the voices you cannot. It is important to decipher what is important and what isn't. Living in accordance with love and the idea that "I am safe" which means "I have nothing to worry about", rather than the natural state which is filled with fear and tribal instincts changes everything. If anger comes up because someone insulted us or yelled at us, this can take over our whole person.

As stated earlier, our nervous systems keep track of everything that happens to us in order to survive today and the future. The main focus of our involuntary nervous systems is survival. Intellectually we can and usually do add a layer of enjoying living and other higher goals of existence. The core of our involuntary function is constantly pushing us to undertake actions and behaviors of survival. This drive is almost more harmful than helpful in today's society (in the developed parts of the world). Our nervous system is always keeping a watchful eye, so to speak, for lions, tigers, and bears.

These days there are no angry animals in our paths but rather acute stress coming from various other areas of life. This is primarily driven by our state of mind and not on the material reality and/or danger lurking in the world around us. The fight or flight response is the response that triggers the release of hormones that prepare your body to either stay and deal with the threat head on, or to run away to safety.

The fight or flight[8] response was first described in the 1920s by a physiologist Walter Cannon. Cannon realized that a chain of rapidly occurring reactions inside the body helped to mobilize the body to deal with threatening circumstances. Today the fight or flight is recognized as part of the first stage of Hans Selye's general adaptation syndrome[9], a theory describing the stress response. What is important to note here is that it happens to everyone under stressful situations.

What happens to you during the fight or flight Response? In response to acute stress, the survival instincts are powerful and can be dangerous. I believe it is time for us to evolve and transcend our survival instincts. Carl Jung wrote, "The natural state of the mind is a self-regulating system that seeks and maintains equilibrium just as the body does." "The natural state of the human mind consists in a jostling together of its components, and in their sometimes-contradictory behavior."

From split brain studies (really "mind"), the new idea emerges that there are literally several selves and they do not necessarily converse with each other internally. Like members of a family, the different minds can work together to help each other, each still having its own mental experiences that others may not even know about, especially when in trauma or after trauma has occurred.

Neurologically, many of the systems of the body have a "control center". Each control center is often attached to an organ. Each organ is run by nerves of that system. For example, the heart is the control center of the cardiac system and is run by nerves that make it pump etc. The liver, stomach, eyeballs etc., all have nerves that make them work. That nervous system is the control center for that system. All of those independent yet interdependent networks are all adjusting to each other and coordinate their efforts through the central nervous system which our brains are a part of. Our brains are the control center for our central nervous system and our brains are the control centers for all the other control centers.

People may also dislike the parts that are angry, destructive and critical. Recognizing that some parts are stuck in the past behavior or even memories, can cause an awareness of understanding and learning new ways of being and even thinking. They may find power and/or safety in anger, destructive or critical thinking. All of this can be let go. Oh, what a relief that can be. Many people want to nurture their own health. The first step is to learn that in everyone, all parts are part of us and deserve love from us, that all of them, even those that are destructive were formed in an attempt to protect the self no matter how much they seem to hurt it.

Our sensory motor neurons which start forming in the last trimester of gestation are the "mouth" of the neurological "river" from which all "tributaries" are formed. In other words, these original neurological patterns are the core blueprint from which we build all our functional and sensory neural pathways for the rest of our lives. They have an effect even if we bury them deeply and do not access them. I discovered a way to nurture them so they can facilitate healthy conscious growth until we die.

The Supermind team uses proprietary reporting methods to see the original patterns emanating from the beginning of our lives and uses them to develop a plan to help people live better lives. Neural pathway patterns in the occipital lobes affect the 12 systems of the body. The perceptions and understandings developed from ages three months to age seven or eight guide the neural pathway neurological creation, attachments and utilization until we change them. These original and core beliefs are often buried deeply in our psyche. This is why we use neurofeedback to show how the nervous system is impacting how we feel and function and to expedite and fortify the change we want to make.

Facing the Pain While Facing the Future

"If you're going through hell, keep going." - Unknown

Nothing is permanent, not even depression and anxiety. Until I created NeuroEmpowerment, there was no quick way to become free from anxiety and depression. There is now a way for many people to get well quickly! With NeuroEmpowerment, many people see life changing results in less than a week. The process of relaxation or just plain getting quiet is something we have not learned to do automatically. Society teaches and rewards the opposite. "Do more!" "Go out there and get the American Dream!" It's counterintuitive to believe you can succeed with little or no effort. NeuroEmpowerment requires relaxation, which is the opposite of expending effort!

Anyone who experiences anxiety and panic attacks knows that they are not controllable when in the middle of them. Unless, that is, you have sufficiently practiced a solution beforehand which you can then apply right before— or during — the anxiety or panic attack.

I began to ask myself what I ask many of my clients today who come to me for relief from their anxiety attacks, for escape from their panic attacks, for freedom. "Is what you believe and feel worth the imprisonment it causes?" Few people realize we are prisoners to our thoughts and beliefs, but this is what my personal experience and my research on treating others has shown me.

During my traumatic time, multiple friends pointed out that life was happening the way it was I had to accept it. Not accepting it for what it was caused me additional amounts of turmoil and pain. As I shared, my emotional pain soon became physical. I developed sciatica, headaches, neck pain, lower back and hip pain. Much of this was caused by my belief that things "should be different."

I had to adjust my belief systems as part of my healing process. I began to accept my circumstances, but because I still believed that what was happening was "wrong" or "bad," it was still causing me huge amounts of pain. I learned that I not only had to accept things, but I also had to let go of my opinions of things.

As I progressed through this traumatic period, I found that many offered help. I would become hopeful and then find out that they could not help me. I learned one of many lessons at this time: When a person is in pain for good reason and you cannot resolve the reason for their pain, it is important to understand that, although nothing you say can fix their problems, a few properly placed words can help.

It is often more meaningful to show up and offer love and support than it is to try to fix people's problems. It is very important for us to communicate clearly what help we need, and on the other side of that, what help we can bring. Make sure that any help offered is in alignment with what they're seeking. Otherwise, the false hope can harm the other person. Providing support and listening is always appropriate but use care when offering concrete help or suggestions.

Like I mentioned in my personal story, I became aware that emotions can cause physical pain. For me, when I thought about my father's hurtful actions and death, I felt pressure around my heart and behind my eyes. When I felt that I was not being respected or was being treated as "less than," the anger came up from around my heart and the lower part of my neck into my shoulders and lower back. When I felt that my worth was in question the muscles around my neck hurt higher up than before. I began to understand more clearly that the emotions I was or was not feeling were causing my muscular tissue to contract. To move from powering through the pain to healing, I had to face the pain and look toward the future.

Continued contraction of any muscle causes pain. Our bodies are always adapting based on what happens in our lives. The more often something occurs, the more that habit or reaction becomes set in our brains and bodies. That is why habits take time to break or change (the science says 21, 30, 60, or 90 days!). It is the daily entrainment of these emotional charges that often causes pain in our bodies.

Our bodies can actually "hard-wire" emotional patterns into our physical tissue. Accordingly, even if after some period of time we stop having the emotion, the emotion may still be manifesting physically in our body. This is why there are multiple modalities which help release these physical manifestations of our emotions. Our state of mind affects our body, both immediately and long term. That is why it's so important to learn how to support our brains and bodies to keep clearing as we work on healing.

Using Sleep to Change

When we are working hard to change negative patterns, it is essential that we have time to integrate those changes. One of the most important times when that occurs is during sleep. Sleep is vitally important. Yet, according to the US National Institute of Health (NIH), 33% of Americans have sleep issues or disorders[10]. I believe that close to 90% of Americans can improve their sleep. This is from my findings from working with over 2,000 people in our wellness center.

I became invested in fixing my own sleep issues and have used the information to help many others. If you're lying awake ruminating about the past, the present, or the future, you are reinforcing the habit of not sleeping. This dynamic often causes a person's nervous system to activate, making it harder to fall asleep rather than decompressing and letting go of the things that are preventing a person from sleeping. When you are physically and emotionally tired, a stress response can destroy sleep and keep you from incorporating any of the healing work you may have accomplished during the day. There are multiple tips for improving sleep in the guide at the end of this book.

Healing is possible; I'm living proof of that. You are already taking steps to feel better just by reading this book. Keep going, even when it is difficult, and make sure you seek out support, be gentle with yourself, and create conditions for ongoing relaxation.

Key Takeaways

Neural Pathways and Fight or Flight Response:
- Early Development: Neural pathway development starts prenatally.
- Fight or Flight Understanding: Our instinctual survival process which is fear based and is often caused by a nervous system misunderstanding and leads to unnecessary anxiety and/or stress.

Impact on States of Mind and Body's Recovery System:
- Influential Factors: Stimulus responses influenced by states of mind, beliefs, and experiences.
- Mindfulness Techniques: Alters states of mind and mental and physical functioning.
- Calm and Relax: Crucial for the body's recovery system and coping with anxiety and stress.

Acceptance and Letting Go:
- Understanding that things are as they are and letting go of how they should be is often crucial for healing.
- Emotional patterns can cause physical pain, requiring release and integration techniques.

Importance of Sleep:
- Quality sleep is vital for integrating positive changes and combating anxiety. Improving sleep quality supports overall well-being and the brain-body healing process.

THE "MIND MAP"

You might remember from my personal story that I was fortunate to find out about a therapeutic tool called Brainwave Optimization. Because it became such an important part of my healing, I spent time studying with the inventors of this method, so that I could incorporate it into the work I do with clients.

The first thing we did with the inventor of Brainwave Optimization was the "Brain Map." (This is technically called a Quantitative Electroencephalogram - QEEG). From this a benchmark of an individual's brain activity is established. As I learned more about the QEEG, I realized that it is a charting of the measurements of the synaptic connections our minds and bodies use to live our lives on a daily basis. The QEEG relies on measurements taken from 12 different placements on the scalp in both resting and interactive states of mind. It is truly amazing what can be determined from this technique.

It is important to note that humans create and utilize electricity which is created through a biochemical reaction within the body utilizing hormones, salt, and potassium. These electrical signals contain the information and messaging system of our bodies. I like to say that our "minds" live in the electricity that we create and utilize in our bodies in order to direct and manage our functioning. Our nervous system has electricity flowing through it when we are alive. Since 2007, I have been studying how we humans function in direct correlation with these electrical signal patterns.

I found that by using neurofeedback equipment and performing an electroencephalograph (EEG) at the same time I can provide graphs of the different levels of the mind. These graphs show how these levels function in the different areas of the brain. This is what is often called a "Brain Map." The chart is like a map because it gives coordinates of different areas of the brain. It shows the functioning levels of the mind in each of those areas and the frequency of the energy waves associated with them. This is why I call it a "Mind Map".

The more clients I saw, the more patterns and energy waves I was able to study. I gained an understanding of how each level of the mind functioned and how imbalances affected my clients. Once we have this information, we can focus the healing techniques to address the specific functions that are out of balance. Because most people probably don't have access to an EEG, I am, at the time of publishing this book, developing a wearable so that anyone struggling with depression, anxiety, or other challenges in their lives can have access to EEG technology and the healing powers of NeuroEmpowerment in their homes.

The profound lesson here is that what we do or say has a significant impact on the consciousness of ourselves mentally and physically and the minds and bodies of others. And the more we understand ourselves the more likely that the impact will be positive. These are the reasons I am writing this book: to help and support others in understanding their own minds and the ways that flawed thinking may be negatively impacting their health and to provide tools for living a more balanced and successful life.

Using the "Mind Map" for myself and in treating others, I now understand that the different layers of the consciousness run all of the different systems of the body. This means the belief systems and the alignment of those layers are extremely important. The neurological connections of each system and their effects are directly impacted by our beliefs in a bi-directional way. This limits our ability to change and evolve as well as gives us the ability to change and evolve.

In fact, sometimes one layer of the psyche takes complete control of the other parts. The unconscious layer is processing the sensory information from our sensory neurons. Its primary responsibility is to process the sensory information as it relates to survival and to run the bodily functions. Accordingly, when we hear a loud noise or a threatening sound, the unconscious activates the fight/flight response mechanisms which may make us jump or start running before we actually know, in the conscious layer of our mind, what is happening.

Studies show that this process can take up to 5 seconds. Due to the fact that the unconscious and subconscious layers form our perceptions, they can shape our understanding of reality. Fight/flight energy patterns are evident on the Mind Map. The patterns often indicate how much of a person's life is wrapped up in these types of survival patterns which often limit our ability to make change or evolve, as mentioned above.

Another very important lesson is that the mind and the brain are two very different entities which can only function together. The brain is the physical structure, while the mind or psyche exists within it as the governing system of thoughts and feelings. The brain and body are constantly changing based on what we demand from them. Sometimes those demands are unconscious, habitual, or rooted in trauma.

In order to change, we must concentrate on the "change agent" that causes the body and its chemistry to make change. In other words, if we demand a certain change in our mind or psyche enough, sooner or later, the brain and body will change physically and chemically in order to facilitate that change, even if we are not consciously making that demand.

This is why deeply ingrained patterns may make change seem

impossible. Remember: these systems work in a bi-directional way. I developed NeuroEmpowerment to integrate psychology, kinesiology, and neurofeedback, along with other methods in order to facilitate change more successfully.

Where do the beliefs that fuel our perceptions, understandings and behaviors come from and why do we stick to them even if they are leading us to our own misery? Our nervous system tracks everything in order to keep us alive. How it functions today is directly dictated by our genetics, epigenetics, our perceptions, and our experiences — everything in our history.

Functionally, as stated earlier, our bodies are equipped with an evolutionary system, called Neuroplasticity, which is basically the science of how mankind adapts. It is the science of how our neurons are formed and connect throughout our nervous system. Every day, we create neurons (Neurogenesis) which imprint our daily experiences into our bodies. These synapses are a part of the nervous systems which in turn are connected to all of our bodily systems. This connection process can take days, weeks or months depending on how much of our lives they affect.

As events happen in our lives (including our own decisions, thoughts or actions), our system decides its importance and then how to "wire" our nerves so that the systems of the body can support and sustain the existence of these events. This is directly influenced by the importance we place on them. These synapses create all the energy and provide all the signaling throughout our bodies and brains. Through Neuroplasticity we learn and retain information our whole lives as well as generate feelings and function.

I break down the layers of the psyche into 4 basic components: unconscious, subconscious, conscious and connections. It is helpful to think of this as a circular process which is bidirectional through the layers of the psyche. These four layers of consciousness and their interaction is pictured on the next page. Think of the process as circular and understand that the process can begin anywhere in the circle.

Levels of Consciousness
Neurological Signals Diagram

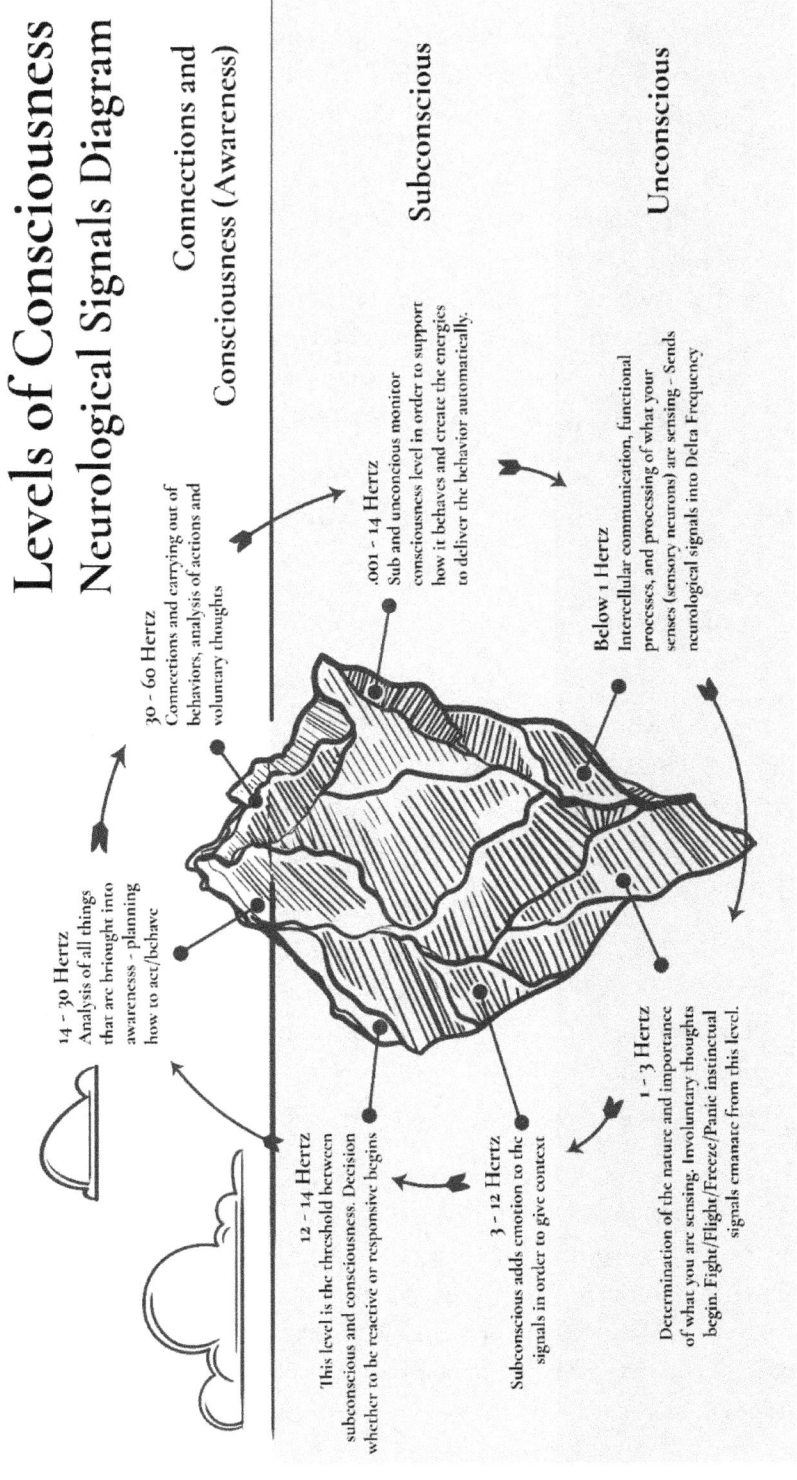

Connections and
Consciousness (Awareness)

Subconscious

Unconscious

30 - 60 Hertz
Connections and carrying out of
behaviors, analysis of actions and
voluntary thoughts

.001 - 14 Hertz
Sub and unconcious monitor
consciousness level in order to support
how it behaves and create the energies
to deliver the behavior automatically.

Below 1 Hertz
Intercellular communication, functional
processes, and processing of what your
senses (sensory neurons) are sensing - Sends
neurological signals into Delta Frequency

14 - 30 Hertz
Analysis of all things
that are briought into
awarenesss - planning
how to act/behave

12 - 14 Hertz
This level is the threshold between
subconscious and consciousness. Decision
whether to be reactive or responsive begins

3 - 12 Hertz
Subconscious adds emotion to the
signals in order to give context

1 - 3 Hertz
Determination of the nature and importance
of what you are sensing. Involuntary thoughts
begin. Fight/Flight/Freeze/Panic instinctual
signals emanate from this level.

1. The *unconscious* runs our bodies and provides signaling into our psyche about how our bodies are functioning as well as the signaling from our sensory systems (eyes, ears, skin, nose, taste buds etc.).

2. The *subconscious* processes the signals coming from the unconscious and/or the conscious layer(s) and decides how important those signals are. It then adds signaling of its own (emotions etc.) of how important the original signals are or redirects the signals to not enter the conscious or unconscious levels of the mind. These signals often are intended to control a person's conscious reaction.

3. The *conscious* mind is what we are aware of.

4. The connections level is where and how we connect with other people, places, or things and connect with the spiritual world.

Each layer of the psyche has its own purpose in order to support survival. This is also true of the different systems and organs of the body. For the purpose of understanding how to manage our anxiety, we have to understand that we are both mind and body and that our existence is a partnership of the two.

It has been said that if you change your mind, the body will follow. Biologically, this is true. As we think, neurons and synapses (connections of neurons) in our bodies are activating and deactivating. So, the old saying that you are what you think you are may be physically true. We can train our bodies to change by changing the way we think.

The body is basically keeping track of what we are thinking, feeling, doing and what is happening around us. This process allows us to create the necessary bodily functions to support and automatically create the "signaling" required for us to survive what is happening. A synapse is created for every event of which our body is aware. If the events which create that synapse are repeated, then other synapses are formed to support the creation of the original synapse.

These synapses eventually connect to all the systems of the body so the body can make that activity (thought, feeling or function) continue automatically. So, at some point, the body begins to generate the thought, feeling or action without the mind initiating it. This is what gives merit to treating the body in order to affect the mind. However, it is my finding that if you only treat the mind or the body, the effects have limited results.

This is why it is vital to treat the mind and body. The body naturally wants to repeat the already created patterns. This is one reason there is such value in journaling, especially if we keep track of how we feel at different times of the day. We often will see very discernible patterns based on bodily function.

Anxiety, as I define it, is always an unintended or unwanted increase in neurological energy. It usually is a fear-based energy which shifts focus and directional energy away from our intentions. This most often occurs when the body follows previously created patterns and the mind is trying to do something different. Our bodies usually drive us to choose our actions based on our instincts and patterns created in our past. If we allow our survival or animal instincts to guide our bodily actions and neurological development, then we are destined to have increasing levels of anxiety.

Our nervous system keeps track of everything in order to keep us safe in the future. The "cosmic joke" is with this being true — live in the now! I like to say that you do not "have" anxiety, because you actually create your anxiety.

We can train our nervous system to "be in the now" automatically. That is the beauty of Neuroplasticity. As our nervous system keeps track of what is happening, it naturally tries to make the patterns of our lives automatic. Therefore, if you have lived with a lot of anxiety, all of your "nows" will automatically have levels of anxiety. Without intentional training to change this dynamic, we behave based on the past, because the nerves we are using now were developed in the past. We can change it so that in a "future now", our nervous system will function more like we want it to with less historical influence. This is why we want to intentionally train our nervous system to function anxiety-free.

Neuroplasticity says we can. This book gives you a track to follow to begin making it happen. You may be gathering by now that this gives a whole new perspective on how to live life.

Understanding Human Instincts And Nervous Systems

To dive deeper into intentionally training your nervous system, we have to understand the interactions of the different levels of our minds. I will address the different levels from the perspective of animal instincts or survival instincts later in the book. When we transcend our survival instincts, we are able to live from a higher plane of human existence, a higher level of humanity. The next stage of our human evolution. This "higher level" of humanity has many meanings. In short, it is to live at a higher level of consciousness.

Another view is regarding the electrical frequencies biologically created in our bodies, when we measure the levels of the mind in the nervous system in hertz (one hertz equals one wave of electricity). The higher the hertz, the higher the level of consciousness. My favorite "higher-level" of consciousness is the state of living from love rather than fear. Because as we shift away from living in fear, which is our natural Homo sapiens state, the average and mean electrical frequencies we create and use rise to higher levels.

The function of the unconscious as it relates to animal instincts is to constantly try to define what is happening around us in order to ascertain if we will survive the moment. Our survival instincts drive us to be in the "pack". Once in the pack, our unconscious has to keep us in the "middle" or front of the pack. Often, once we have perceived we have gotten there, we quickly find out that it is almost impossible to stay there. Since all the other members of the "pack" are trying to make their way to their favorite position in the pack, the positions are always in flux.

If we move to the front of the position in the pack, it is perceived that the other members of the pack will give us favorable attention and even take care of our needs. Unfortunately, we find that other people are trying to pull us down so they can move to the front of the pack themselves. Remember, this "thought" process is at the instinctual level, so many of us are not aware of it. However, if you pay attention, whenever we perceive that someone is "better" than us, more respected or liked than us, etc. then we tend to tear them down in thought, word or deed. There are several writings that describe varying levels of this phenomenon. Some call this "herd instincts". The word for Homo sapiens packs or herds is a "tribe". Accordingly, I call these tribal instincts.

It is my opinion that tribal instincts are at the root of most of the problems in the world and why divorce rates are climbing over 50%. Unless entrained differently, these tribal instincts prompt our nervous system to provide constant information (functional and emotional) as if our survival depends on it. The signaling defines our position in the tribe and monitors how those in and out of our tribe behave and treat us. We get automatic warning signals if members of the tribe behave in such a way that "threatens" our position in the tribe. These signals trigger fight or flight reactions within us because, unless otherwise altered, our nervous system considers our inclusion and position in the tribe somewhat life threatening.

If the information is coming from a person outside our tribe, we get warning signals for fight and flight reactions to move us into "tribal warfare" because for survival in the tribal dynamic, those around us MUST behave and treat us in accordance with our perceived tribal rules and customs or they are literally threatening our survival and we should kill them (maybe to extradite them from the tribe or demote them to a much lower level in the tribe) or avoid them at all cost. With this dynamic comes the NEED for respect, a NEED for loyalty and a huge fear of abandonment. None of this is necessary for survival in today's society. They are all nice things to have, and we may want them and enjoy having them in our lives, however, they are not NEEDED for our SURVIVAL.

At Supermind, our psychological/executive coaching and neurological entrainment services are geared toward elevating our humanity above these instinctual dynamics which are pervasive in our world today. We have found the neurological algorithms which exhibit the instinctive animal behaviors and the ones that provide for mature, responsible, rational, empathetic, and compassionate behaviors. The responsible, rational, empathetic, and compassionate behaviors are housed in the level of the mind which utilizes more waves of electricity per second a.k.a. higher frequencies of electricity or higher frequency bands. Accordingly, we are actually helping people to live in the "higher" frequencies, thus, a higher level of humanity.

We have been using a neurological "lens" while watching the psychological wellbeing of our patients improve. We have also codified (created a numerical representation of) the neurological components of psychological wellbeing. This is why at Supermind we say, "We've cracked the code to a more conscious you" and that we are "Your path to better brainwaves".

Our process of NeuroEmpowerment allows us to break down the different parts of your consciousness and lay them out for you so you can decide what components of your psyche you want to heal, change, love, and nurture (or just omit from your neurological processing). We then provide the guidance and use the neurotechnology to facilitate you making the desired changes and incorporating them into your daily living as quickly as possible.

As far as we know, as of the printing of this book, this is performed faster at Supermind than any other place in the world. Further, using neurotechnology, we measure, monitor and track each person's progress for safety, precision, and efficacy and to further the science of NeuroEmpowerment.

For deeper understanding, it is important to acknowledge that as the unconscious is constantly surveying what is happening around us, the subconscious lets us know the significance of what we are sensing and defining in the unconscious. This significance is portrayed through emotions. The more significant the unconscious subject matter is, the stronger the emotion. The subconscious also decides what is worthy of awareness in the conscious mind. This is a learned response. When emotions are coming into consciousness, our system tries to react based on our "history" of reacting to whatever is causing the signal.

As the emotional flow moves into consciousness, we choose to accept or deny the emotional content of the thought, word, or deed. Whatever we do, the more we do it, the more our body conditions itself (and our nervous system) to automatically create the energy for those thoughts, words or deeds. Many people talk about the autonomic nervous system (called the ANS). It is important to know that we can influence how the autonomic nervous system functions by training it accordingly. I purposely did not say that we can train it to function properly. "Properly" in medical terms provides very different definitions than what I am looking for. The ANS is said to run our fight/flight instincts and our involuntary bodily functions. To function properly medically, it is doing that. We could be functioning on "auto-pilot" not paying much attention to what is happening around us, and the ANS could be functioning properly.

There is another nervous system called the somatic nervous system which governs our bodily functions in order to allow our input. This system is known for our voluntary functioning. Our ANS may have very little involvement with our somatic nervous system. We may have an extreme amount of anxiety. We may be surviving just fine. Medically everything would be "proper". Living this way would make it very hard to enjoy living. I am done just surviving. I am very concerned with the level of involvement of my ANS in my everyday life. I want my ANS to be very interactive with my somatic nervous system. I work every day to lower the effect of my fight and flight instincts on my daily functioning. In this way, I can focus on the voluntary function of enjoying living which leads to and maintains anxiety-free living.

Another characteristic of the animal's instinctual subconscious drive is the constant surveying of what is happening around us in order to define our surroundings. This is part of the herd instinct, the drive to be pack-animals. I further realized that this drive existed at the lowest levels of my psyche and directly affected my bodily functions, like digestion, sleep and energy creation (adrenal system). Many people were telling me to get control of myself and my life, which is the ultimate desire of defining our environment. I realized that this was impossible, especially when my sleep patterns were my number one problem. I did not then know that a solution was near at hand that would change my life and embark me on this journey of living anxiety free.

In every culture, there are unwritten rules which provide the path to climbing the echelons of society which are drummed into all of us by the media, well-meaning parents, teachers, and institutions. For example, some of the beliefs are, "In order to succeed in life you must make a lot of money, have a big car, and work your head off," and "boys are to be big and strong and dare not cry!"

Having to always act like we are "supposed to" simply causes excessive amounts of anxiety or stress. From this, our ANS is trained to always be fighting (or flighting), which in turn can cause constant anxiety. There is a reason that they call the assets a man acquires and surrounds himself with "his trappings". Eventually, confusion and too much stress, fear, and depression can interrupt the ability to thrive. The good news is that the damage caused by fear, pain, anxiety, stress, and old beliefs can be overturned. The best news of all is that everyone can learn how to be the person they have always dreamt of being.

To get there (being the person you want to be), requires analyzing and changing your B.S. Yes, I am talking about your belief systems (BS). BS may not be the terminology you prefer. I am not sure if there is proper terminology to describe the understanding, perspective, entrained instincts or functional capabilities of subconscious and unconscious functions. I call them the belief systems of our psyche and our biological systems. Each level of our psyche and bodily systems have a different set of BS (belief systems) by which they function on a daily basis. These belief systems "direct" our bodies on how to function.

For example, If my subconscious believes I am a good guy who does good things for people, then my lungs are breaking down my air to give me the energy to be a good guy, my stomach is breaking down my food in order to give me the nutrients necessary to be a good guy etc. Even more importantly, my neurons are demanding the hormones necessary to create the electrical impulses in order to fuel my nervous system to generate the energy and function so I can be a good guy.

Hopefully, you have learned and become aware now that your path to the you that you have always wanted to be has already begun. It began with your cry for help (I like to think, the buying of this book). It began with your new awareness that you can drastically influence your mind and body so that you can become the you that you really want to be. It began with feeling overwhelmed and stuck. It always begins with facing your fears. You might still have some confusion and doubt. In your process, your path to the you that you want to be may require support from others who believe in you and your possibilities!

Through our clientele at Supermind, we have documented that the different layers of the mind (Conscious, Subconscious, and Unconscious) have their own operating systems (belief systems) in the physical realm, namely the nervous system, which work autonomously while still being oscillating interdependent networks. In other words, each level of consciousness actually affects the body differently. The functions of the body are broken up into 12 different systems. According to some they are the following:

1. **Circulatory System/ Cardiovascular System**
   - Circulates blood around the body via the heart, arteries and veins, delivering oxygen and nutrients to organs and cells and carrying their waste products away
   - Keeps the body's temperature in a safe range
2. **Digestive System and Excretory System**
   - System to absorb nutrients and remove waste via the gastrointestinal tract, including the mouth, esophagus, stomach and intestines
   - Eliminates waste from the body

3.   **Endocrine System**
      - Influences the function of the body using hormones
4.   **Integumentary System / Exocrine System**
      - Skin, hair, nails, sweat and other exocrine glands
5.   **Immune System and Lymphatic System**
      - Defends the body against pathogens that may harm the body.
      - The system comprises a network of lymphatic vessels that carry a clear fluid called lymph
6.   **Nervous System**
      - Collects and processes information from the senses via nerves and the brain and tells the muscles to contract to cause physical actions
7.   **Muscular System**
      - Enables the body to move using muscles
8.   **Renal System and Urinary System**
      - The system where the kidneys filter blood to produce urine, and get rid of waste
9.   **Reproductive System**
      - The reproductive organs required for the production of offspring
10.   **Respiratory System**
      - Brings air into and out of the lungs to absorb oxygen and remove carbon dioxide
11.   **Skeletal System**
      - Bones maintain the structure of the body and its organs - (I add; this is where our blood is made - in a process called hematopoiesis.)
12.   **Sensory Systems - and their interconnections**
      - Eyes - seeing, ears - hearing, taste buds - taste, skin - touch etc., nose - smelling

If we are not managing our intentions of how these processes work, then they will form in haphazard patterns. These systems physically govern how we feel, function, think, and behave until we live from a higher-level of consciousness. If we are feeling lost or confused about what we have been doing or how we have been feeling, lack of intentional direction of these systems may be a large reason for that. Lack of differentiation of "needs", "wants", and "likes" is a simple commonality that has become glaringly obvious from all the people I have worked with. As stated earlier, beliefs cause our bodies to function in different ways. Accordingly, it is important to intentionally choose our beliefs (and when to apply them) regarding "needs", "wants", and "likes"

Needs vs. Wants for Present Day

Abraham Maslow realized this and wrote about basic needs that we all have. Maslow's hierarchy of needs, illustrated on the following page, has the presumption that what we need most is to satisfy our physical needs of food, warmth, and love. Deprivation of these basic needs will cause a stall in mental growth and pursuit of future goals. Also included in the physiological needs are warmth, clothing, sex and sleep. According to Maslow, if these needs are not satisfied, the human body cannot function properly.

The next needs to be satisfied are safety needs. For example, security order, law, stability and freedom from fear. The next need is for love and belonging. The need for interpersonal relationships motivates behavior. Examples include friendship, intimacy, trust, and acceptance. receiving acceptance and love, sexual intimacy, being affiliated with others, family friends and work. The next level includes esteem for self, dignity, achievement, mastery, independence, and the desire for respect from others, that is status and prestige.

I have and am reworking the Maslow Hierarchy of Needs. The Cole's Trapezoid of Needs changes things a bit. Maslow's writings regarding this pyramid progressed and changed a bit over his lifetime. My version will probably change a bit over time also. So, I am calling this version the 2024 Cole Hierarchy of Needs. In the Cole version, we are reworking the pyramid. Because survival needs are rarely in question, our biological survival instincts get confused.

What gets in the way is how we manage our needs, wants, and likes. The bottom two tiers of Maslow's are now one tier in a trapezoid which contain the basic requirements in order to survive.

Here this is called The Survival Needs Tier, and the next tier becomes the Animal Instincts Tier. That is the extent of the Cole Hierarchy of Needs pyramid. The higher tiers become the Hierarchy of Human Consciousness development (likes and wants). These tiers start with the Enjoyment of Living Tier, and the second tier becomes the Self-actualization Tier and top level becomes the Transcendence Tier.

Maslow's Hierarchy of Needs

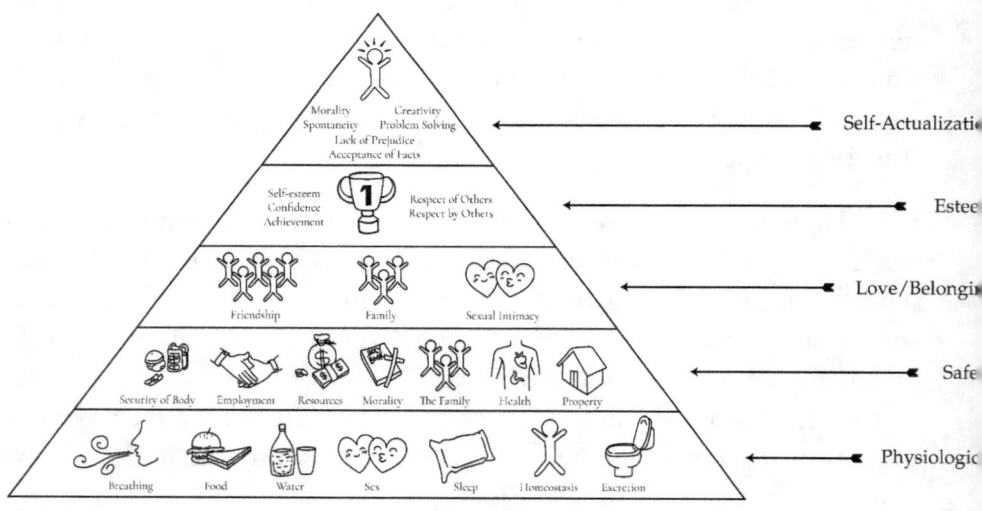

This Survival Needs Tier (Physiological) includes attaining and maintaining air, food, water, good safe shelter for sleep, moderately good health and a means to get rid of our trash and excretions.

The next level, the animal instincts tier (safety), are needs such as security for our body, financial support or equivalent resources, a good moral code, and a society or tribe.

Those are our Homo sapiens needs. The higher tiers Maslow was speaking of are for being happy, which I am suggesting that we do not "need" to survive.

The first tier of the hierarchy of human consciousness (enjoying living) includes understanding the difference between needs, wants and likes and how to enjoy living.

The second tier is accessible after the first tier and is basically an automatic part of living that requires extremely little energy on a daily basis.

The third level of this tier is the transitioning into enjoying the fruits of existence and increasing identification with meaning and love.

The Cole Trapezoid

When I was introduced to the Maslow needs hierarchy, I was taught to move from the bottom toward the top through the pyramid, and to ask myself the question for each level; "Are these needs met for me?"

One major reason that I created The Cole Trapezoid was my experience with fulfilling the Maslow Pyramid. In this process of intentional living I realized that the levels of my psyche were very confused. I believed that breaking my depression was a basic need that had to be conquered because if I did not conquer it, I might have ended up killing myself. Through my experience, I realized that by releasing it as a need, I was able to free up more energetic resources which I could then use to be happy. Through my experience with Maslow's Pyramid, I created The Cole's Trapezoid in order to align the neurological levels of my psyche to create more alignment with my intention which automatically reduced my anxiety. This also paved the way for a better understanding of the importance of each level of the psyche as it is represented on the "Mind Map".

My experience with Maslow's first and second tiers (physiological and safety - the real needs) caused me to directly define "What do I need, or what am I lacking today?" Here are some examples: Do I have enough food today, enough water? Am I sleeping enough? I was taught to pay attention to the basic psychological needs. Without those, I was told that I could not be fully equipped to get what I needed on the path to the me that I wanted to be.

Programming the Reactive Mind
to be Responsive

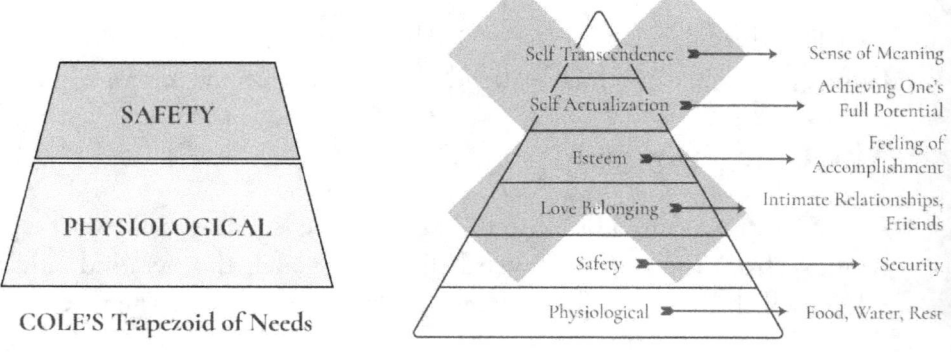

COLE'S Trapezoid of Needs

MASLOW'S New Hierarchy of Needs

The trapezoid shows true needs
Everything else is a want, like or desire!

I soon realized that getting these needs met was not really a concern at all. I could basically do nothing and these needs would be met on the day in question. This was and is true because I have always been very "productive" and am in a society and place that allows me to easily attain the "needs" of the first and second tier.

I have come to realize that I am a little bit privileged because of this. I also realized that this was important for me to be grateful for and that my body, more specifically, my nervous system, was wasting energy worrying about my basic needs. In other words, when I realized that I was safe and that I really did not have to worry about getting my needs met, I realized that all of my worrying about those issues was a complete waste of time and energy. I then set out to get my system to stop trying to make me worry about those kinds of things. This was much easier said than done. It has been an ongoing journey for the last two decades of my life.

At this point, I had become very practiced at cognitive behavior and mindfulness techniques. I applied these on a daily basis through daily meditation and self-direction. As I stated earlier, my number one problem was my sleep patterns. A byproduct of my sleep was depressive thinking. So, I created a daily practice which allowed me to apply techniques daily that helped me counteract my sleep issue and become happy by the end of the day. I call it my "Morning Mental Fitness Routine". I would (and still do) get up two hours early in order to implement this routine which consists of the following:

- Breathing and meditation - When I first began to do this, my mind was always racing with "1000" forms of fear. So, I would begin by breathing and meditating in order to quiet down the fear based stream of consciousness which was a root part of my depression. The breathing technique I used, use now, and teach is to breathe in to the count of 3, hold my breath for the count of 3, and then breathe out for the count of 3. The counting is at a comfortable pace (it does not have to be seconds) the important part is the focus on the. Breath and the counting. When focus on this other thoughts (or anxieties) are hard to think about (there are lots of different breathing techniques, I advise you to try different ones and use whichever works best for you. My meditations has changed a lot over the years. One I have used often to quiet the "thousand thoughts syndrome" is to imagine is am lying on the beach and if another part of my mind interrupts, I have a conversation with that part if be a say "I am meditating about the beach, I want you (that part of my mind) to be the palm trees." I would then go back to meditating and if another thought interrupted, I would then assign it to another part of the beach scene (the waves, wind, porpoises etc.). It read my beach in my mind - I create it to be peaceful, beautiful, happy, and calm (anxiety free). I would (and still do) then focus on the happy and peaceful feelings and direct my nervous system to keep creating those feelings as my ongoing unconscious "default" feelings. I soon learned that this breathing and meditating was a good warm up for my fitness routine which allowed me to create a "happy consciousness."

- Praying and asking for help - In the beginning of this practice, I was told and learned it to be true that prayer and petition were great ways to guide my inner, unconscious self, to direct my energy in the "correct" direction. I also would journal and keep track of my prayers and petitions which allowed me to see that many of my prayers "were answered". If the answer was "yes", I was very pleased, if the answer was "no" or "not yet", I usually was able to see a good reason for that to be the answer. The benefit of the saying that "hindsight is 20-20" was amplified by my journaling of my prayers and petitions because I could go back and reread my journal and see how everything played out. Through this practice I soon saw the value of prayer and petition.

- Physical grounding and fitness - The next part of my routine became walking barefoot into my butterfly garden and practicing Xi Gong, stretching and working out on my workout equipment in my house. Keeping a healthy mind and body is important. This is also a great opportunity to direct my body how to better serve my mind.

- I then drink alkaline water (water with lemon juice) and then head to my bubble bath for reading spiritual works, journaling and meditation.

They say that the first thing you have to do to "get out of a hole" is realize you are in a hole. I soon realized that I was spending a lot of my time, unnecessarily allowing my unconscious to create anxiety worrying about my survival needs being met when they were already met and, based on how I was living my life, would continue to be met for a long time.

I began to add into my meditations a reaffirmation that all my needs were met. My intent was (and is) to train my unconscious part of me that is run by animal instincts not to waste any energy concerning myself with how to meet my survival needs.

As shown above, my unconscious tries to control me with fight/flight/freeze/panic to make sure I survive. I can handle my survival (except for biological health) from my intellect. I am done with allowing my involuntary fight/flight/freeze/panic instincts to be "on" all the time. In my daily life, they no longer serve me.

To live anxiety and stress free it is important to lower the energetic levels of these types of neurological activities to a minimum. It is important to manage the survival instincts from our intellect. These instincts are a waste of energy for most of us most of the time. These instincts can be turned "off" and "on" through self-directed neuroplasticity-based mindfulness exercises and lots of repetition (practice). This way, when we choose to be or are placed in situations where these instincts are necessary or important, we can turn them back on through setting our intention.

The four animal instinct responses I have presented are also depicted in other ways. Recently "faint", "fawn", and "friend" have also sometimes been used when describing the acute stress responses that I am referring to as the animal instincts. "Faint" is another way to describe the "flight" response. The "flight" response does not necessarily mean run away, it is more about avoiding and or withdrawing. In this context "Faint" refers to an extreme withdrawal (possibly with excess drama included). "Freeze" is the next level beyond "flight" or "faint". The terms "fawn" and "friend" in this context are interchangeable with "fight". "Fight" is used to describe the instinctual drive to put the gas pedal on and show to handle things as well as actually fight. So, when a crisis or situation arises that triggers our stress response in a social situation, "fawn" and "friend" describe the reaction of stepping forward and fawning all over someone and/or being friendly in order to attempt to manipulate, control, and/or diffuse a situation.

In my nomenclature I stick to fight/flight/freeze/panic as broad descriptions of instinctual stress responses because there are many specific techniques which fall within the four categories and just listing the four mentioned can be applied to the other descriptions and many more.

In order to experience Maslow's Third tier (love/belonging) and to navigate, grow from, and better understand my experiences, I learned to have phone numbers of five people I could call at any given time to discuss what I was thinking. I would call the five people until one of them picked up, and I shared with them what I was thinking and feeling.

It was important to find people with whom I was not emotionally attached. This helped them to be able to provide objective opinions of my experience. These five people guided me to resources to fill any unmet needs, helping me fulfill the first two tiers of needs until I was fulfilling them myself. Even though (actually much like my family) there was no emotional attachment, interacting with these people helped me feel loved and like I belonged.

This was a tier of learning for me. I did not fully understand love. I knew how to become accepted by groups and "belong". Because I had little understanding of love, this was a work in progress for many years and is too in depth to tackle here.

As a part of learning more about love I began to follow directions from spiritual books as they related to love. I soon found that it was really important to love myself fully in order to be able to love others and receive love. By following these "formulas" for living and continuing my Morning Mental Fitness Routine, I began to see in my journaling what kind of man I was becoming. I found out if I lived a "righteous life" I became a "righteous man". This brought me through the fourth tier as I built my self-esteem.

As I followed this formula for living, began to feel better, and built my self-esteem, I began to help others that were struggling with similar issues begin to get better. I have devoted my life to helping the world become a love-based place one world (each person's "world" is housed in their nervous system) at a time. This tier includes self-identity (and actions) becoming synonymous with perception of purpose.

The fifth tier, often called self-actualization, is where humans move into enjoyment of the manifestations of our purpose and the development of ourselves in alignment with our purpose.

I really created the Cole version to differentiate from Maslow's Pyramid because I realized that many of the problems people experience are due to the involuntary nervous system confusing needs, wants and likes. Maslow's pyramid treats them all as "needs". This inclusion in Maslow's pyramid has and may extenuate the confusion.

Most of my "needs" were "needed" in order to keep me safe. So, the next big question was "Am I safe?"

Another realization I had was that most of my actions were intended to make me safe. I realized that I was taking these actions when I was already safe. Accordingly, most of those actions were entirely unnecessary. Regarding survival, I realized I have nothing to worry about, and likely neither do you. The main problem is that too many of our involuntary functions are concerned with keeping us safe when we are already safe most of the time.

After looking at tens of thousands of brainwave maps, I am certain that it is a natural Homo sapiens instinct to be overly concerned with safety at the lowest part of our psyche. Fortunately, this level of consciousness (and our nervous system) can be retrained. In this book, I am guiding you to intentionally interact with your unconscious nervous system to allow you less involuntary survival processing and more voluntary processing so you can thrive instead of continuing to just survive. It is time to stop "just hanging in there" or "just getting by".

Many people's confusion regarding "needs" and safety are due to limiting beliefs which guide all levels of our psyche on how to function. The belief that causes many people to create extra anxiety is that their wants are their needs. In other words, they believe that what they want is something they need. The unconscious understands all "needs" as something that is needed for survival. So when people see their wants as their needs, they are adding lots of extra survival concerns to their unconscious systems daily function. This causes extra and unneeded anxiety. As we change our belief systems our levels of anxiety change.

The ability to feel safe with other people is probably the single most important aspect of mental health. Safe connections are fundamental to meaningful and satisfying lives. Many studies of disaster response around the world have shown that social support is the most powerful protection against becoming overwhelmed by stress and trauma.

Key Takeaways

Unlocking the Power of Mind Mapping:
- Mind Map Creation: The Quantitative Electroencephalogram (QEEG) sets a mental activity baseline.
- Understanding Brain Function: Neurofeedback and EEG help chart and interact with multiple mental levels and functions.
- Healing Insights: Mind Maps inform tailored healing techniques.
- Self-Understanding: Discover how self-awareness positively affects consciousness.

Understanding Our Human Instincts:
- Elevate Your Humanity: Transition beyond survival instincts for higher consciousness.
- The Unconscious and Survival: The unconscious level of the mind's primary concern is survival. It often tries to control us through the fight and flight mechanisms which may be entirely unnecessary for us in this day and age. To live anxiety free, we want to minimize the survival mechanism and maximize the enjoyment of living mechanisms.
- The Influence of Tribal Instincts: Tribal Instincts cause tribal warfare and tribal hierarchies. In the developed world, these are more often damaging rather than helpful.
- Supermind's Approach: Promote empathy, responsibility, and rational behavior through NeuroEmpowerment.
- Path to Change: NeuroEmpowerment transforms your consciousness
- The Subconscious's Role: It assigns significance to sensory input emanating from intra-cellular impulses, impacting emotions.
- Navigating the ANS: Train your Autonomic Nervous System to reduce fight-or-flight instincts.
- Belief System Transformation: You can alter belief systems to induce physical changes.
- Your Self-Improvement Journey: Is a journey into Self-awareness, change, and mastering of mental and bodily systems.

Key Takeaways

Needs vs. Wants in Today's World:

Maslow's Hierarchy of Needs:

- Understand the pyramid of physiological, safety, love/belonging, esteem, and self-actualization "needs."

Cole's Hierarchy of Needs:

- Simplify "needs" to only include health related and critical animal survival instincts.
- Then enjoying life, self-actualization, and transcendence become wants, likes and desires.

Human Consciousness Development:

- Ascend towards happiness and higher consciousness.

The Morning Mental Fitness Routine:

- A practical daily regimen to intentionally affect involuntary thinking and nurture happiness through mind-body synchronization.

Taming Survival Instincts:

- Train your unconscious not to fret over fulfilled survival needs.

Needs, Wants, and Likes:

- Differentiate them to reduce anxiety.

The Power of Safety:

- Create an environment where you feel secure for better mental health.

MENTAL WELLNESS TREATMENT ALTERNATIVES

The issues of anxiety, depression, and overall mental wellbeing is a multi-billion-dollar industry, and millions seek treatment every year, so what makes Supermind NeuroEmpowerment the best, and worth trying? In order to discuss the alternatives, I am breaking down mental wellness into four different categories: mental health, cognitive performance improvement, neurological issues, and longevity. NeuroEmpowerment helps all four categories of mental wellness listed.

"Helps" means that it lessens the symptoms or eradicates the factors which cause the diagnosis listed. "Helps" can also mean that it improves performance in the listed category. Supermind NeuroEmpowerment is a standardized process and the only modality that measures if and how much it helps objectively as well as subjectively, so it can be distributed with consistent and sustainable results across multiple distribution sites.

Category One – Mental Health issues

Mental health issues include and are not limited to the following –
- Agoraphobia
- Anorexia Nervosa
- Any Anxiety Disorder
- Any Mood Disorder - Depression
- Attention-Deficit/Hyperactivity Disorder (ADD and ADHD)
- Autism Spectrum Disorder (ASD)
- Addiction Issues
- Eating Disorders
- Generalized Anxiety Disorder
- Panic Disorder
- Persistent Depressive Disorder (Dysthymic Disorder)
- Post-Traumatic Stress Disorder (PTSD)
- Serious Mental Illness – Bipolar – Schizophrenia - Psychosis
- Any Phobia
- Suicide
- Anger -Rage Issues
- Excessive Frustration
- Sleep Issues
- Fear Based Disorders
- Self-Identity and/or Self-esteem Issues
- Low Emotional Intelligence
- Tourette's Syndrome Stuttering
- Many other Syndromes

Category Two – Cognitive Performance Improvement
- The ability to improve intellectual capabilities.

Category Three – Neurological Issues
Issues with the nervous system including and not limited to,
- Fibromyalgia
- Dementia
- Neuropathy

- Asthma
- Alzheimer's
- Tourette's Syndrome
- Some forms of Chronic Pain

Category Four – Longevity
- The medicine of aging well in order to live a longer and happy life as we get older.

Treatments for the above categories include and are not limited to Talk Therapy (Psychology), Physical Therapies (Some include mental therapy – yoga is a good example), Psychiatry, medicine (prescribed by doctors), plant medicine (psychedelics), religion – spiritual healing, neurofeedback, EMDR (binaural beats and other bidirectional eye movement type therapies), 12-step programs and alcohol or drug rehabilitation centers, transcranial magnetic stimulation (TMS) and MeRT therapy. There are so many different types of therapies that all could not be included here.

NeuroEmpowerment stands apart from all of the listed modalities because it actively treats the mind and the body at the same time with a singularity of purpose, which is to align the mental and physical parts of the body to optimal personal, mental and physical health. This process helps all of the above categories. Another key component is that NeuroEmpowerment objectively measures the neurological (state of mind) state of our patients throughout our therapeutic process. A more specific comparison of NeuroEmpowerment and the other listed modalities follows.

Talk Therapy and Physical Therapy

These therapies include working with a psychologist, some psychiatrists, a life or executive coach, a wellness coach, a personal trainer, and many other types of coaches (religious guides are listed elsewhere and not included here) whether in person or through "Telehealth".

Talk therapy begins with finding a good match with a therapist. Finding a good match can take anywhere from 1 day to 1 year. Talk therapy begins with a history of the case which can take one to five hours. This history is rarely complete, which causes more work to be performed in this phase of the therapeutic process. Within this "history" phase of the process, certain professionals will perform testing and provide a diagnosis. In general, coaches are not allowed to perform (depending on licensing and regulatory policy) "therapy" or provide "diagnosis" as a part of their process.

I include personal trainers in this section because many provide advice as to how to improve mental as well as physical health. Supermind provides this form of therapy through licensed mental health counselors (LMHCs) and limited medical advice through medical doctors (MDs) who are on the staff. All information is kept confidential to the Supermind staff unless otherwise directed by our clients. Talk therapy along with physical (neural) therapy are integrated in the Supermind NeuroEmpowerment Program.

Talk therapy and physical therapy very rarely help in all four listed categories of mental wellness. They will often help with one to three of the categories, however, the results are all subjective. Due to the subjective nature of these therapies, they cannot be provided with consistent results at multiple distribution sites.

Treatment via Medications

Doctors and psychiatrists prescribe medication to help with mental health issues. Medications prescribed for mental health issues do not heal or fix the underlying mental health issues. They may or may not temporarily correct a "chemical imbalance" which may or may not be causing the issue. This is why most of the time when the doctor or psychiatrist prescribes the medication, they say things like "this has been found to help with" or "let's try this and see what happens".

Another unfortunate happenstance with medications is that they often cause side effects. If doctors were truly prescribing the medications to correct chemical imbalances, it would make sense for them to actually test a person's chemical balance before prescribing the medication. It's unfortunate that chemical balance testing is rarely performed before medications of this nature are prescribed.

Medications may help in all four categories; however, one medication will almost rarely help all four categories. Accordingly, to get help in all four categories one may have to take four medications and then hope and pray that they do not interact with each other or the person in a negative way. Medications are often referred to as a band aid approach because their effect is temporary.

Since chemical balances are not tested on a regular basis and there is not an established cross reference of the chemical balances to the mental function, there is no objective measurement of treatment success. Accordingly, the science and the results are purely subjective and not reliable across multiple distribution sites.

Supermind does not engage in the practice of prescribing medications. Supermind coordinates care with the physicians who prescribe medications. Supermind hopes to collaborate with pharmaceutical companies to create digital programming which accomplishes the same results as many medications.

Meditation

There are many forms of meditation which are useful in many different ways. Meditation has been practiced for thousands of years in many different cultures. Meditation is more of a form of self-maintenance and self-care than a "treatment". There are mental health interventions which incorporate meditation as a technique which can facilitate and further treatment effectiveness. Different forms of meditation have different effects on the people that use them. Knowing the effects of each form of meditation on the mind and body is important when deciding which type of meditation to do, the length of each meditation session, and the regularity of sessions. There are types of meditation which are more specific for certain heritage and cultural genetics.

I have come across many people in my practice who have told me that they meditated on a regular basis and yet were still facing challenges with control of their ability to be present. When I was able to ask more specifically about their meditative practices, I typically could help them change how they were meditating in order to gain more control over their presence. Properly planned and implemented, meditation is a powerful tool which can and often does support mental health treatment and, more significantly, ongoing maintenance of mental health, which is why Supermind incorporates and integrates several forms of meditation practice in the NeuroEmpowerment Program.

Yoga

Yoga is much like meditation in that there are many forms of yoga with varying effects on the mind and body. Pretty much everything that applies to the discussion of meditation applies to yoga. However, yoga has a much more pronounced physiological effect than mediation alone. Many consider yoga to be an advanced form of meditation.

Supermind program of integrating breath with neurological change may be considered a form of yoga (maybe not). However, NeuroEmpowerment and yoga have intentional breathing techniques, self-direction, and physiological change in common.

Thai Chi and Qigong And Other Forms Of Martial Arts)

Thai Chi and Qigong along with other forms of Martial Arts are all important methodologies for creating synergy and balance between the mind and body. All of these forms of self-maintenance and self-care have been used for centuries and have been proven to have significant effects on the health of the mind and body. It is rare for one methodology to be utilized as a treatment or support mechanism for all forms of mental health. These forms of mental health therapy or practice are useful as a "part of life" which helps avoid mental health problems in the first place. If problems arise, having a basis in these methodologies provides a rich framework for intervention as well as healing. Supermind is as similar to this as it is to Yoga.

Plant Medicine

Plant medicines have been utilized for hundreds of years as a form of mental health analysis, treatment, and spiritual growth practice. Spiritual teachers, guides, seekers, artists and athletes have also been known to experiment with plant medicines in order to improve performance and or the ability to be more "deeply connected" within themselves and with whatever they wish to connect with that exists around them.

There are those that attach identities to the plant medicines themselves, making them a true mental and physical intervention. Some say the "mother" plant will guide the user to the lessons they are to learn. There are many studies regarding plant medicines. There are just too many "unknowns" in this field at this time.

There are also significant risks inherent within the use of plant medicines. Many of the active components of many plant medicines are not understood and their effects on the physiological and psychological connection relational to human function is often unknown. Many people have experienced life-altering, permanent side effects from using plant medicines. Unfortunately, the science around the use of plant medicines is not sufficient to assure safe usage at all times.

The idea that a person might "need" a plant medicine can insinuate that they cannot heal their mental function on their own and require an outside force to make the necessary change. It is many people's opinion that this is a limited view and that humans can heal on their own. So, utilizing plant medicine as a "required" form of change may create an untrue dependency. Further, plant medicine is often taken in groups in a ritual or ceremony. The group can directly affect the experience of the individual and may cause an individual to not be able to heal due to shame or other dynamics caused by the group.

Supermind does not engage in the utilization of plant medicine, however, Supermind will coordinate care. Further, Supermind hopes to collaborate with shaman and/or pharmaceutical companies to create digital programming which could be considered a digital form of the medicines that fall under this category.

Religious, Spiritual, And Energy Healing Modalities

For thousands of years religion, spiritual guidance, and energy healers have been a part of helping people with their mental health. Unfortunately, the results of the modalities and methodologies vary widely among practitioners and end-users.

These forms of healing are very subjective in treatment protocol and measurement of outcomes. This means that the results of these modalities cannot be relied upon as replicable and valid for study. This limits the widespread acceptance of these forms of modalities. The effectiveness information is typically anecdotal and validated through testimonials and referrals, which limits the ability for the types of modalities to grow widespread acceptance. This means that there are fantastic stories of miraculous healing, yet, just because it seems to work for one person, there is no assurance that it will work for many other people.

Typically, advancements take a lot of time in these modalities. They also may require some devotion to their cause. Supermind has developed a protocol which utilizes much of the doctrine and practices of this category which can be used if the patient desires it.

Neurofeedback

Neurofeedback is a modality that has been around since the 1960s and has proven to be effective in numerous studies. John Lennon and Yoko Ono were big advocates of Neurofeedback. However, the treatment protocol is very subjective to the practitioner administering the treatment. The results are also very subjective for the patients.

Unfortunately, Neurofeedback is a medical procedure dealing primarily with the body with the hope of affecting mental health, without having a model of optimal mental health. The closest model this modality has is "normal" based on the brainwave frequency thresholds.

Most Neurofeedback practitioners utilize z-score training which is based on a normative database. Normal does not really work anymore. So, in my opinion, if you are seeking better function for a specific disorder, Neurofeedback can help. Otherwise, the results are very subjective and, without some sort of psychological treatment performed while doing the Neurofeedback, not lasting or sustainable.

That being said, there are plenty of conscious people who really understand what they are looking for and how to use Neurofeedback therapy to have good results. Supermind gives feedback of neurological function via isochronic tones and visual feedback. That is where the similarities of NeuroEmpowerment and classic Neurofeedback end.

EMDR, Binaural Beats And Other Bidirectional Therapies

Eye Movement Directional Therapy and Reprocessing (EMDR) is a therapy discovered in the 1980s which is extremely effective for releasing trauma and recovery therapy. The mechanism of the therapy is to force the brain to process from side to side and back and forth until it becomes unstable. At this point, the nervous system reverts its processing mechanisms to the last known "survival" or stabilizing pattern, which is typically before the last trauma. This therapy is very effective for many people. There are many different ways to perform bi-directional therapy other than through "Eye-Movement". Another form of EMDR therapy is "Binaural Beats". Unfortunately, many people use binaural beats for extended amounts of times and repetitions without the "Reprocessing" part of EMDR. This type of therapy is not intended to be utilized for long periods of time especially without the reprocessing part of the therapy.

Supermind utilizes its own form of bidirectional therapy within the neural therapy part of NeuroEmpowerment. Supermind will also occasionally use EMDR in the psychotherapy part of NeuroEmpowerment. Judi Pasos, LMHC, a core part of our team, is an EMDR specialist. Unfortunately, people who have never had a stable processing state usually have very limited positive results from EMDR or other forms of bi-directional therapy. Accordingly, Supermind only uses this therapy in a very controlled environment and in a limited way when it is appropriate.

12-step Programs and Alcohol and Drug Rehabilitation Centers

12-step Programs have been around since the 1930s and have been very effective for those that become a part of the new, sober lifestyle offered in the support groups. The 12 steps provide an easy-to-follow guide to altering how a person lives their life.

Typically, these programs offer and provide the ability for members to guide the newcomers. This allows people who have "been there before" to guide those that are in the throes of addictions to living addiction free. "Sobriety" is often rooted in guiding others and giving back to the program by being a part of the meetings and helping others. The programs are extremely effective, however, the statistics show that less than 10% of those who are introduced to 12-step programs become recovered.

The following sources document the statistics and give more information regarding 12-step programs.

1. Alcoholics Anonymous. *Historical Data: The Birth of A.A. and Its Growth in the U.S./Canada.*
2. Alcoholics Anonymous. (2017). *This is A.A. An introduction to the A.A. Recovery Program.*
3. Substance Abuse and Mental Health Services Administration. (2018). *Key Substance Use and Mental Health Indicators in the United States: Results from the 2017 National Survey on Drug Use and Health.*
4. Substance Abuse and Mental Health Services Administration. (2017). *Behavioral Health Barometer, United States, Volume 4.*
5. Alcoholics Anonymous. *2014 Membership Survey.*
6. Lilienfeld, S. and Arkowitz, H. (2011). *Does Alcoholics Anonymous Work? Scientific American.*
7. Stein, J. and Forgione, M. (2011). *Charlie Sheen claims AA has a 5% success rate – is he right? Los Angeles Times.*
8. Friedman, R. (2014). *Taking Aim at 12-Step Programs. The New York Times.*
9. Alcoholics Anonymous World Services, Inc. (2001). *Alcoholics Anonymous: The Story of How Many Thousands of Men and Women Have Recovered From Alcoholism.*
10. Kelly, J. and Yeterian, J. *The Role of Mutual-Help Groups in Extending the Framework of Treatment.* National Institute on Alcohol Abuse and Alcoholism.
11. Kaskutas, L.A. (2009). Alcoholics Anonymous Effectiveness: Faith Meets Science. *Journal of Addictive Diseases, 28(2), 145–157.*

Alcohol and Drug Rehabilitation Centers also are successful approximately 10% of the time for first time patients. The industry seems to perform extremely well partly due to the fact that many people receive treatment from rehabilitation centers multiple times.

Supermind has been successful at helping people beat their addictions more than 50% of the time. Studies are being commissioned in order to provide evidence-based documentation of this fact.

Transcranial Magnetic Stimulation (TMS) And MeRT therapies

TMS and MeRT therapies are promising therapies which are medically based and primarily focus the treatment on the physiology with the hope of affecting the mental function of their patients. These treatments have shown effectiveness in many cases. Their best efficacy is in cases where the physiology of the patients is compromised in some way. When the physiology is compromised due to a psychological condition or process, then these treatments have less effectiveness.

NeuroEmpowerment treats the mind and body and therefore will be more effective for a greater number of people. However, people whose physiology is compromised will be effectively treated by TMS and MeRT. Combining treatments is also extremely effective. Collaboration with the TMS, MeRT, and NeuroEmpowerment providers is highly encouraged and will increase the effectiveness of the treatments.

This is a limited scope of alternative therapies yet still covers the majority of what is available. Overall, the available treatments for mental health and psychological well-being have not yet been quite as effective as NeuroEmpowerment.

Key Takeaways

Mental Health Spectrum:
- Diverse Range: Encompasses anxiety, depression, bipolar, schizophrenia, and psychosis as well as many others.
- Varied Treatments: Traditional methods include talk therapy, shock therapy, medications, Neurofeedback, and alternative modalities.

Cognitive Enhancement:
- Intellectual Focus: Has been utilized for improving cognitive abilities without specific methods.

Neurological Challenges:
- Comprehensive Approach: NeuroEmpowerment addresses mental and physical aspects of many disorders, including fibromyalgia, dementia, and chronic pain.

Longevity and Well-being:
- Holistic Aim: NeuroEmpowerment aligns mental and physical health for optimal well-being and potential longevity.

Alternative Modalities Overview:
- Integrated Therapies: Talk and physical (neuronal) therapy integrated into NeuroEmpowerment.
- Medications Caution: Often prescribed without comprehensive understanding; addresses symptoms temporarily.
- Mind-Body Practices: Meditation, Yoga, Tai Chi, Xigong and many other practices contribute to self-maintenance and mental well-being.
- Plant Medicine Consideration: Historical use but caution due to unknowns and risks.
- Religious-Spiritual Healing: Subjective with varying results; Supermind incorporates select practices.
- Effective Neurofeedback Integration: Supermind blends isochronic tones and visual feedback driven by intentional mental function.
- 12-step Programs Impact: Limited success rates, Supermind reports over 50% success in addiction support.
- Physiological Approaches: TMS and MeRT focus on mental function through normative physiological treatment.
- Collaborative Approach: Encourages collaboration with TMS, MeRT, many other therapies, and NeuroEmpowerment for comprehensive results.

THE APPLICATION OF BIOFEEDBACK

Biofeedback is any methodology which provides feedback to the body in vivo (in real time or live time). Biofeedback can be used diagnostically by professionals with the training and license to diagnose and to help train the body to function differently. Neurofeedback is a form of Biofeedback.

You have been learning about your body and mind activating the fight or flight response. One way you can ease your stress and overwhelm, even your anxiety is through Neurofeedback. Technically, Neurofeedback is an operant conditioning-based technique in which individuals sense, interact with, and manage their own physiological and mental states. Since we are both mind and body it is very nice to be able to treat both the mind and body in one application.

Biofeedback is a mind and body technique that involves using visual or auditory feedback to gain control over involuntary bodily functions such as heart rate, muscle tension, blood flow, pain perception and blood pressure. The process involves being connected to a device with sensors that provide feedback about specific aspects of your body.

A major goal of biofeedback and neurofeedback is to make changes to the body that result in a desired effect psychologically. As I have said many times, we are both mind and body. Accordingly, I like to involve both the physiology and the psyche when using biofeedback, so I often include neurofeedback or do a little neurofeedback before and then after the biofeedback training. This might include relaxing certain muscles, slowing heart rate or respiration or reducing feelings of pain.

A variety of instruments can monitor heart rate, for example when in the midst of a fight or flight response under danger or stress. It has been measured and statistics have shown that induced relaxation and the learning of how to get to the desired relaxed state of being can actually cause your body to ease and go back to being emotionally and physically able to get out of danger to yourself.

Over time, these changes can endure without continued use of instrumentation. In the case of migraine or muscle tension headaches the blood rushing to the heart and head can even be recalled through relaxation to flow once again evenly over the body and the headache is relieved. Blood pressure can be measured, a relaxation takes place, and the instrument monitoring shows the high levels of blood pressure being reduced. Self-regulation is just so beautiful that the relaxation can restore your comfort with yourself. It's great to know that can happen and then feel the results. Now, contemplate that all of this is driven by thought (the mind).

Neurofeedback works by providing a different perspective and way to react to physical signs and symptoms of stress and anxiety. Scientists have proven (both in Supermind and outside of Supermind) that it is often the stress response, the tendency to go into a state of fight or flight in order to decrease potential threats, that can actually exacerbate certain conditions. So, learning how to control physiological responses to stress through neurofeedback can often improve overall health and help you to learn how to relax your mind and body.

Neurofeedback training can also be used as one part of a treatment, sometimes to augment medication. You can learn many things through neurofeedback including how to either manage the stress you feel in the face of feelings of anxiety, or handle stress that results from another condition. I created neurofeedforward to take the biofeedback and neurofeedback a step further. Through intentional and mindful self-direction while utilizing the neurofeedback equipment, we can stop creating the unnecessary or unwanted fight and flight responses rather than just learning how to cope with them. You can above all learn to take charge of your health, which allows you to feel more in control, and less overwhelmed.

Neurofeedback is a subdivision of Biofeedback[11]. In fact, many people's first reaction to hearing the term "neurofeedback" is to ask me, "Do you mean biofeedback?" — which they have heard about at some point in their life, especially if they once owned a "mood ring."

Simply put, biofeedback is a method of gaining information by monitoring skin temperature, blood pressure, heart rate, brainwaves, and other body conditions to help promote control over normally involuntary bodily processes through conditioning, also called operant conditioning[12] and relaxation.

Biofeedback is a general category. There are several types of neurofeedback: heart rate variability (HRV), thermal (as seen in a "mood ring" or a thermometer), muscular (EMG), and neurological (EEG) — also called neurotherapy, neuro-biofeedback, or neurofeedback. That is why I am providing a short list (not all-inclusive) of them here with explanations of how they can be useful.

All forms of biofeedback employ some type of computer or monitoring device along with electronic sensors to give information about what is going on in the body. With neurofeedback, it is giving feedback about specific brain waves: the percentage amount of each one in specific areas of the brain, called amplitude, readings showing how well the brainwaves work harmoniously together (regulated or balanced), or if not working well together, there is dysregulation (imbalance).

When the brain is dysregulated or imbalanced, it is like a symphony orchestra tuning up, making a lot of noise that is unpleasant to the ear. Another example I give is that after you drive down a road and hit a pothole, one tire is now out of alignment with the other tires. Because of the misalignment, your car is no longer working as efficiently as before and it might even make it harder to steer the car.

Also, using the example of your car, anyone who needs a yearly state inspection knows that the car is hooked up to various computers to see if the engine or transmission is working properly. The newer forms of neurofeedback also provide this type of information. It is now possible to map out the brain through quantitative EEG (QEEG) or identify specific regions of the brain that are not working properly. These are called the Brodmann Areas. Still, other forms of neurofeedback provide information on how your brain compares to others of the same gender and age. This is done through Z-score methods.

Just as your mechanic will inform you of the condition of your car, neurofeedback provides information about your brain. Once an assessment or evaluation has been done, you can use a wide variety of neurofeedback methods to fix a specific area, and/or dysregulation or just fine-tune it, as you can do with your car's engine.

Some people, after getting their car inspected, have the skills to go home and do their own repair work. So, too, with neurofeedback — some types of neurofeedback do not need experienced clinicians to help. However, just like you might have had a friend or neighbor who said they could fix your car only to make things worse, this too has been part of the history of neurofeedback. Some people have bought equipment without proper training or understanding of the brain and have made symptoms worse by not using the equipment properly.

I developed NeuroEmpowerment which is a complete protocol to affect neurological change with the intention of creating the optimal psychological outcomes possible utilizing neurofeedback in an advanced way that we call Neurofeedforward. Our system has a three-pronged semi-redundant aspect which provides higher levels of safety and quality assurance. Furthermore, our methodology teaches ongoing mindfulness techniques so our clients can benefit from the advances they make with Supermind for the rest of their lives just by continuing to apply the techniques in their daily lives.

Why Use Biofeedback Or Neurofeedback

One of my favorite questions I get asked is "If Neurofeedback is so good, why is its use not more widespread?" The answer to that question has many layers. My favorite part of the answer is that I have discovered a different way to use the Neurofeedback and other forms of Biofeedback. People have been using biofeedback for hundreds of years in order to learn heart rate control to reduce anxiety and stress, but my variation defines what is ailing so many people and what is holding so many people back from living at a higher level of humanity. Another reason is that it has so many uses that standardized procedures and the science behind it have not yet (until now) been created to allow medicine and science to fully understand how to use it.

During the relaxation treatment the patient is asked to visualize as vividly as possible a variety of stressful situations while attempting to maintain the relaxed muscle tension, or at least to be able to recover quickly from an increased tension resulting from the visual image. The patient at this time is encouraged to transfer his or her tension control, learning to control real-life stressors, and to try to relax after stressful situations.

With neurofeedback, and practice of relaxation, the patient is actually learning the art of controlling anxiety. Even more exciting, the patient is creating neural pathways that they did not have before which give them the ability to self-regulate the anxiety; eventually not creating it at all. This study[13] is one of the many that show that trying to force anxiety to go away often has the opposite effect.

Psychophysiologic studies, particularly relating to stress, anxiety, and arousal, show that easing heart rate activity can be easily achieved and that heart rate is a sensitive indicator of emotion and autonomic reactivity. The relationship between heart rate and subjective feeling states has been dramatically illustrated in many neurofeedback experiments.

Heart rate, heart rate biofeedback and neurofeedback are exquisitely sensitive to cognitive factors. It has been found that the more kinds of information about the process that are available, the more rapid and more effective is the learning to control heart rate. It is to be expected that human beings have some sense or awareness of heart rate activity, since often they can feel their pulse pound or race. But by the time a person feels their heart pounding they have missed out on the ability to use self-regulation to prevent the creation of anxiety or stress.

Learning to control heart rate is a relatively easy task, however, it requires on-going practice and repetition. For example, the heart rate is generally faster in anxiety states, yet when the anxious individual listens to a slow heartbeat and is told that it is their heart beat, their own heart rate can slow and their subjective anxiety decreases. In this light, heart rate neurofeedback learning may contribute substantially as a preventive technique, allowing individuals to learn to suppress inappropriate heart rate reactivity and maintain an optimal functional state with minimal effects of stress. Relaxation training and practice on a daily basis is essential to strengthening the ability to avoid stress and anxiety and/or manage it if they arise.

Brainwave Feedback (Neurofeedback) And Controlling Stress

Certainly, cerebral electrical activity of human beings is a great potential resource for understanding the dynamics of all human behavior. Neurofeedback is the biological feedback which allows "access" to the mental systems which drive how the brain interacts with, the nervous systems of the body, the skeletal muscle activity, the activity of organs, and the systems of the body. Human beings can learn to control a wide variety of extraordinarily complex brain and body functions.

I have been helping people gain more awareness of how their mind can reprogram their brains and bodies to serve them better for decades. Throughout the history of brain and body research, the difficulties of relating brain function to mental activity have been blocking the advancement of this exciting field. NeuroEmpowerment and The Mind Quant are providing the data from a more objective framework which will help advance the field of mental health treatment significantly.

We use psychological coaching and brainwave feedback (Neurofeedback) to produce, sustain, and control brain states and accompanying mind states conducive to many different emotional, mental, and functional states on a sustainable basis. As stated earlier, brainwave patterns as measured through EEG technology reflect a dynamic range of mental and physical activities. They, the brain and body electrical activities, are the energies given off as the brain and body neurons process sensory and motor information, feelings, or functions. As the brain and body process information of a perceptual, sensory, memory, experiential, or judgmental nature, the sum of these activities is measurable, through the active neurons.

We have discovered that the vast majority of all psychological issues (and many physiological) and disorders are produced by imbalanced nervous systems and that when we help people align their nervous system into a balance that serves them, most of the psychological and many physiological issues cease to exist. An example of this is the relationship between alpha brainwaves and pain.

The use of the electroencephalogram or EEG is used to record brain rhythms at the most relaxed state which can often produce an alpha state (state where alpha occupies the highest percentage of all brainwave proportions in a location). It is used widely to register states of stress electrically in the brain at which time the patient can learn to relax while the feedback from the EEG helps the patient being recorded "see" and feel that they themselves are reducing their stress. It shows control, not by force, but by essentially teaching the mind and nervous system to be quiet and through changing thoughts and practicing how to achieve a more relaxed state. Once calm, thoughts may be redirected toward new decisions leading to the process of success and the willingness to change unwanted behaviors that are no longer useful.

Some reports on experimental clinical uses of alpha feedback reveal two consistent and significant themes running throughout all studies. The first includes a psychological process which turns the attention of the minds of patients inwardly. This reduces the amount of attention paid to external factors and leads to a decrease in mental tension or rumination about social pressures. This effect alters the significance that the individual attaches to external environmental situations. This effect is a mental change accompanied by a higher volume proportionately of alpha brainwaves.

The second significant theme the various clinical reports discuss is the importance of the *idea* of self-control which develops during the training and that is used by the patient as a motivating factor, facilitating the learning process. In other words, the patient learns self-control. Even more astounding is that the patients learned how to be in control and feel tranquil within one week. I have personally been involved professionally (as the creator and a practitioner of NeuroEmpowerment) in this process with thousands of people. This is a very common experience at Supermind. This is why we have so many five-star reviews.

Retrain Your Muscles for Desired Functioning

Relearning motor (muscle) skills can be very challenging. For example, the adult attempting to relearn roller skating or whirling a hula hoop. In the past adults have long been indoctrinated with the concept that determined effort is the essential ingredient for success. When it comes to manipulations of the body's physiological functions that have been put on automatic for so long, there can be difficulties in recapturing the childhood ease of just letting muscle systems adjust themselves and work how we want them to.

This is also true in the case of nerve-muscle problems, where patterns of muscle activity designed to compensate for deficits or protect against pain, have replaced the normal muscle activity. It is a complex problem involving forgotten or substituted learned patterns that are linked to surprisingly dominant higher mental influences.

These factors are why in the case of retraining muscles or organs to a new desired function it is not just determined effort which is necessary. Repetition during many repetitive days is the key. Our involuntary nervous system and our physiology learn habitually, meaning from our daily activity over an extended amount of time (21 to 90 days).

When relearning, extra energy and effort are required because we are going against past patterns and physiology, undoing past neurological connections and building new tissue. The patient can become easily fatigued. This is a mental and a physical fatigue as the habitual patterns take over. Also, the anxiety of effort prevents or interferes with motor unit activation. Circular thinking and circular neurological patterns are often developed throughout our lives for extended periods of time which makes breaking them even harder.

The problems of anxiety and fatigue that occur during the muscle rehabilitation process can be relieved by including relaxation in the treatment program. It is not simply the process of converting the almost automatic reflex into voluntary control. As recovery proceeds, new motor units become active and flutter in and out of the pattern, and these too, must be brought under voluntary control.

Biofeedback muscle rehabilitation training requires a patient and therapeutic approach because it consists of coaxing two problems into a productive resolution. One problem is activating motor units while the second is teasing their activity away from unproductive patterns. Together these objectives are directed toward useful, normal activity. Neurofeedback is useful in this process also. While we think, our bodies are building physical neural pathways to complete the tasks we are thinking of. We can harness this part of neuroplasticity to enable us to condition our system to provide what we desire.

Migraine Headache Prevention

As researched and reported by Hans Selye around 1950, stress[14] plays a major role in physical health and in the onset of migraine headaches. Physiologically when under stress to the point of executing the "fight or flight" response, blood leaves the hands and feet and rushes to the major organs and adrenalin is pumped in as a matter of general adaptation to stress.

Remember that our frame of mind, opinions and belief systems are the driver of the physiological responses. When we have anxiety and/or stress, blood vessels constrict and then reopen again in the head and heart to give major strength in the major organs. Those who feel the onset of either too much stress or the beginning of a headache can learn the relaxation techniques and prevent the onset of a migraine headache.

This doesn't happen overnight but with practice of learned skills and the use of autogenic training. My findings are that this is very useful. However, it returns us to a state where our animal instincts are still in charge of neurogenesis and the rest of the neuroplasticity phases, without much intentional direction from our intellect. Accordingly, we integrate this kind of training with intellectual guidance techniques. Often a thermometer showing temperature is used as feedback in the training process.

Thoughts and visualizations of a warm sun or a warm bath can allow the blood rushing to the head to return to the hands and feet preventing a pounding headache. This can be accomplished by relaxing and self-direction. When it is working well the feedback shows that the temperature is rising in the extremities. It has been scientifically measured. The patient can often be weaned from their medication.[15]

Blood Pressure Measurement

Essential (primary) hypertension occurs when the hypertension is not related to any physical issues. This clearly means that it is due to a psychological issue. In order to correct this type of hypertension many people develop behavioral patterns by which they avoid stressful situations or become overtly relatively unreactive.

Evidence suggests that hypertensives are often personalities which contain high amounts of anxiety, fear, hostility, anger, or aggression. The interpretation is made that such individuals do not process their psychological issues well, and that in turn activates those nervous system mechanisms which constrict blood vessels. It could be a person who wants to fight back, but who cannot. It would then logically follow that a majority of essential hypertensives would benefit to some degree by stress-reduction (I like to add: stress avoidance) treatment techniques (as described herein). Certainly, here the target is relief of the tension of the blood vessel muscles themselves, or equally as likely a general reduction in body tension.

Essentially, hypertension or not, persons with hypertension can benefit from reducing or avoiding stress and anxiety. Biofeedback can be useful in helping people with hypertension learn and implement techniques to reduce their anxiety and/or stress.

Temperature and other forms of neurofeedback training for vasomotor activity control, can alter the amount of medications necessary. Caroline Yucha from the University of Nevada conducted a study[16] which found that 60 percent of the patients responded by significant reductions of blood pressure and in 20 percent, medications could be discontinued.

Alpha Feedback And Pain Relief

It is well known and multiple studies have proven that there is a circular interaction between anxiety and pain, and that each tends to increase the other until one or the other is relieved. In the past, pain killers have been exclusively used (and in some cases, over used) with many side effects. As demonstrated by Shimizu et al. (2022) in their study[17], chronic pain patients who received alpha wave neurofeedback training, in addition to cognitive behavioral therapy and physical therapy, showed changes in the amplitude of alpha waves, an increased tolerance to pain, and reduced reactivity to emotional situations, thereby mitigating the pain.

NeuroEmpowerment provides a very simple "lesson plan" for people to follow in order to learn how to reduce many brainwave imbalances. The lesson plan is augmented by a proprietary form of Neurofeedback (Neurofeedforward). Often, once the patient begins to feel the shifts and gain control of their feelings, their physical appearance often changes. They no longer look like very tense and rigid people and appear lax and happy instead.

These shifts come with an awareness that a certain amount of self-healing or self-control as well as shifting belief systems and perceptions is a large part of achieving their goals and becoming who they want to be. This also often comes with a feeling and an understanding that new directions and new decisions aid in improved internal processing of most illnesses whether in the body or in the mind. Our process helps people develop hope instead of depression, calm instead of anxiety enlisted from the inside of every patient which produces renewal and recovery.

Alpha frequency training is a big part of the NeuroEmpowerment process. Utilizing the data and experience of thousands of people, we have developed specific algorithms of optimal alpha frequency proportions for people to feel happier, healthier, and whole. I have had the privilege of helping more than two thousand people improve their moods and learn how to live more stable lives and be happier on a daily basis.

Neurofeedforward

"Symptoms" come with nervous system imbalances which originate from a combination of mental and physical causes. Therapy is a partnership between patient and therapist. The key is communication, the exchange of information. In its simplest expression the caregiver, doctor, or therapist provides information and the patient performs.

NeuroEmpowerment adds another treatment partner to this dynamic, Neurofeedforward. It is most effective when the therapist and patient have a solid understanding of the neurofeedback process, why it can be effective, what its critical elements are, and possibly most important, that they are working with a quite different human capability than believed existed. This is a large part of the "lesson plan" which is utilized to help people make life changing transformations at Supermind.

In the first years of life, we learn and practice things like rolling over, then crawling, then standing and walking and so on. All this was learned and practiced in order to perform purposefully. The entire process is internal and self-actuated through our amazing nervous systems. NeuroEmpowerment is similar because it is a learning and practicing process. The patient must and can learn how to control their internal biology in the same way they learned control over muscle movements. They then immediately practice what they have learned through the course of their daily lives.

Mirror neurons and our sensory neurons mimic those in our environment which help the internal process. Our nerves will often conceptually or physically "try-out" what we sense in our environment. If we like it and/or it works for us, then the self-actuation is completed. Neurofeedback and Neurofeedforward provide a model that activates the mirror, sensory, and motor neuron networks (neuropathways). The therapist's/doctor's task is to have a clear understanding of what kinds of information the patient needs in order to reprogram or program their internal function.

NeuroEmpowerment takes this a step further by teaching the client to identify with themselves and to "program" themselves to live in full alignment in future circumstances. This also enables them to undo their "issues" which have blocked them from being able to live as their best selves.

When totally "stressed out," most of us have had the experience of not having the capacity to think clearly! So, we rely on old behaviors and old beliefs that no longer cause us to be who we really want and need to be. But we don't know how to change so that we no longer go down the proverbial "rabbit hole". The best part of all is that we can eliminate our stress and fear. We can change our behaviors to achieve what we really want! We can redesign our thinking from "I can't do this" to "I CAN!" We can change our beliefs which change our perceptions, which in turn change how our involuntary nervous system reacts to stimulus.

In the turmoil of stress or panic, we often forget what we really want and who we want to be. We can become blocked and shut down. Learning biofeedback and neurofeedback can condition the nervous systems to react differently, in a relaxed way, to reach the goals we so desire. So, there is hope. Just like when we first learned to walk, this is a learning (and practicing) process that is perfectly natural for our minds and bodies to incorporate into our lives.

Key Takeaways

Biofeedback and Neurofeedback Essentials:
- Real-Time Feedback: Biofeedback provides instant feedback to the body, while neurofeedback focuses on neuronal activity (usually in the brain).

Stress and Overwhelm Management:
- Neurofeedback Benefits: Provides ability to rewire the brain and nervous system directly affecting involuntary bodily functions as well as many other mental, emotional, spiritual, and physical functions.

Mind-Body Integration
- Comprehensive Approach: Biofeedback addresses both mind and body simultaneously, using sensors for specific physiological feedback driven by mental function and the mind-body symbiosis.

Changing Physiological Responses:
- Inducing Desired Changes: Biofeedback alters physiological responses through mental interaction, such as relaxing muscles and reducing pain perception.

Enduring Changes and Stress Response Control:
- Sustained Effects: Biofeedback-induced changes can persist over time, offering relief from conditions like migraines.
- Controlled Stress Response: Neurofeedback provides a different perspective on stress symptoms, aiding in symptom management.

Augmenting Treatment and Neurofeedforward:
- Complementary Treatment: Neurofeedback complements medication, equipping individuals with stress management strategies.
- Fight-or-Flight Prevention: Neurofeedforward prevents unnecessary stress responses, empowering individuals to take control of their health.

Key Takeaways

Types of Biofeedback and Assessment:
- Various Forms: Heart rate variability, thermal, muscular, and neurological biofeedback address specific conditions.
- Neurofeedback Assessment: Provides information on brain function, allowing targeted methods for improvement.

Safety, Quality Assurance, and Muscle Retraining:
- Essential Training: Proper training is crucial for safe neurofeedback.
- Comprehensive Protocols: Programs like NeuroEmpowerment incorporate mindfulness for lasting positive outcomes.
- Muscle Retraining: Overcoming ingrained patterns requires repetition over 30 to 90 days, managing fatigue with relaxation techniques.

Why Use Biofeedback or Neurofeedback and Alpha Feedback:
- Historical Roots: Biofeedback and neurofeedback tap into historical roots with recent transformative potential.
- Creating Neural Pathways: Neurofeedback and relaxation practices create new neural pathways, controlling anxiety.
- Alpha Feedback for Pain Relief: Disrupting anxiety-pain cycles through alpha feedback aids pain relief.

HOW NEUROEMPOWERMENT DIFFERS

Why do we resist change? There are a few reasons. First, our involuntary nervous systems primary purpose is survival. Accordingly, it is constantly creating neural pathways so we can survive. For survival reasons, the involuntary system will shut down the voluntary system. This is the basis of the Amygdala Hijack described by Daniel Goleman in his 1996 book *Emotional Intelligence.* Accordingly, the involuntary system does not entirely trust the voluntary nervous systems to make the right decisions to survive, so the involuntary system takes over. In an anxiety or panic attack or depression, we may lose faith in ourselves. We can see that we are in a stressful situation and yet we can't make a clear decision on what to do next. Often, this incongruence is caused by disparity between the involuntary and the voluntary nervous systems.

Another reason we may resist change is that our involuntary nervous system needs time to make change and we are trying to make the change too fast. If we do not have the neural pathways to do something, then we cannot do it. We may struggle to perform new behaviors just because we do not have the neural pathways to perform said behaviors. This often looks like and feels like resistance.

Neurological signals diagram
Subconcious Filtering – Resistance

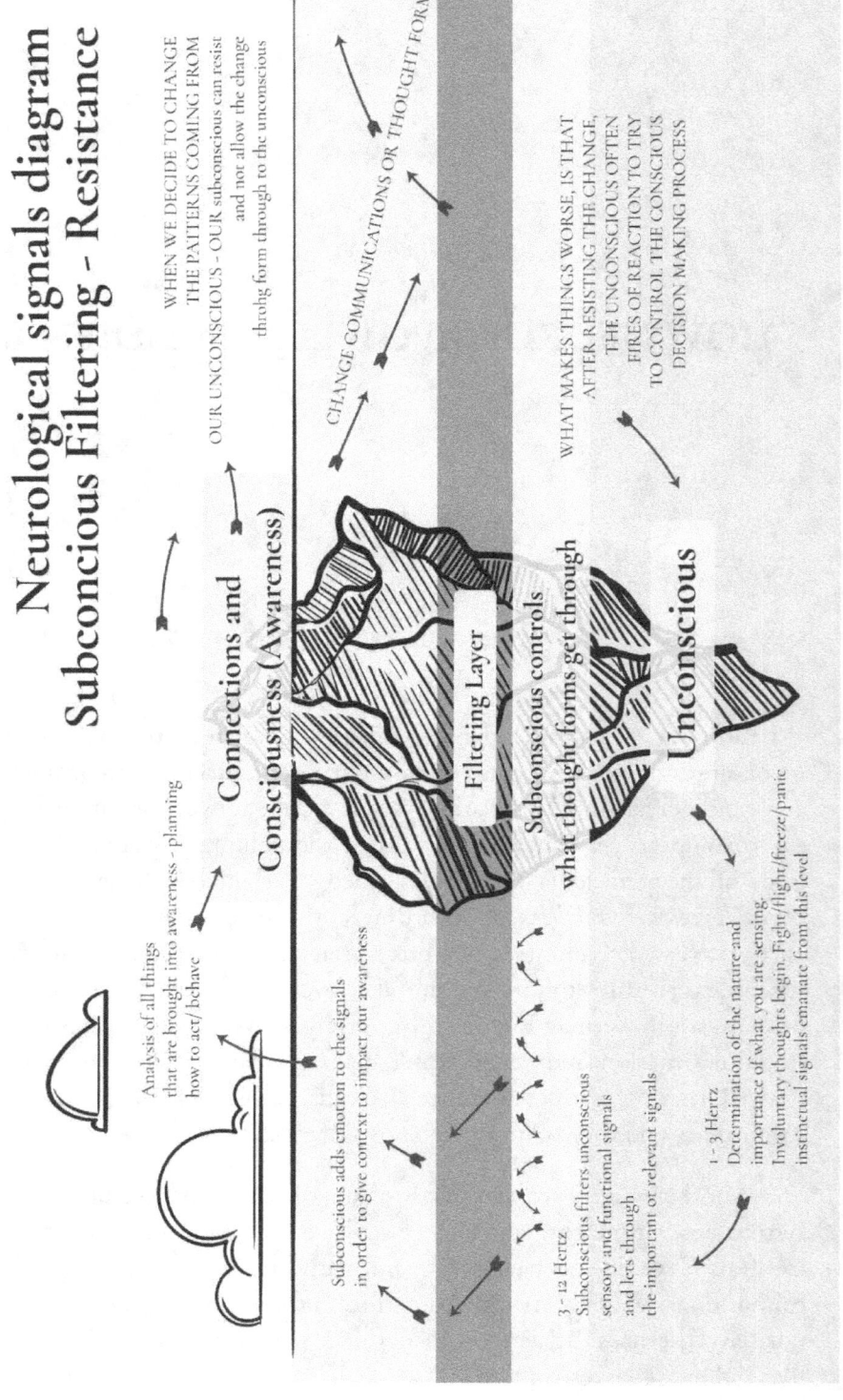

WHEN WE DECIDE TO CHANGE THE PATTERNS COMING FROM OUR UNCONSCIOUS – OUR subconscious can resist and not allow the change throhg form through to the unconscious

CHANGE COMMUNICATIONS OR THOUGHT FORM

WHAT MAKES THINGS WORSE, IS THAT AFTER RESISTING THE CHANGE, THE UNCONSCIOUS OFTEN FIRES OF REACTION TO TRY TO CONTROL THE CONSCIOUS DECISION MAKING PROCESS

Connections and Consciousness (Awareness)

Filtering Layer

Subconscious controls what thought forms get through

Unconscious

Analysis of all things that are brought into awareness - planning how to act/behave

Subconscious adds emotion to the signals in order to give context to impact our awareness

3 - 12 Hertz
Subconscious filters unconscious sensory and functional signals and lets through the important or relevant signals

1 - 3 Hertz
Determination of the nature and importance of what you are sensing. Involuntary thoughts begin. Fight/flight/freeze/panic instinctual signals emanate from this level

Another reason why change is resisted by our system may be that our involuntary nervous system learns based on habitual actions. There are 12 systems of the body which create neural pathways to support new behaviors. This takes time. These neural pathways are created and strengthened based on repetition, preferably on consecutive days or as close together as possible. That is one of the reasons it is said that it takes 21 to 90 days to change a habit.

Biofeedback, Neurofeedback, and especially Neurofeedforward speed up these processes of change, allowing us to dive deeper into the psyche and deepen the effect within our bodies. This is extremely valuable, because speeding up change actually means that the change is easier to implement into our lives and sustain. This is occurring because the feedback systems enable us to compress the time it takes to create more neural pathways. Building neural networks more quickly reduces the chances that the body's defense mechanisms will block the change. The audio mirroring and direction of our neural pathways through the neurofeedback mechanisms guide the body to change the neural pathways, anchoring the changes deep in our psyche and our bodies.

Let's go back to the original dilemma. We are stressed. Our bodies are in pain and we are overwhelmed. We have the old beliefs that we should keep on striving in the same old way that we have in the past. When we do that we become even more stressed out. So, we get stuck! Stuck means that we are overwhelmed. Overwhelmed means we don't know what to do to go forward in our lives. Maybe we have even forgotten what we want! Why? Because we have lost faith in ourselves. Our self-worth, self-esteem, call it what you want, is impaired.

In this instance, our involuntary nervous system has won. Out of fear or multiple fear driven concerns, our involuntary nervous system has succeeded in shutting us down. This shut down helps our involuntary nervous system feel more in control, safer, and often more powerful. It seems kind of ridiculous, however, that it is the same response that causes animals to freeze. The freeze response is exactly what I am describing here. It is part of the flight response. The opposite response is the fight response. Both are driven by our involuntary nervous system.

We don't want to tell anyone how we are feeling because we are ashamed about what we are dealing with, and we are FEARFUL of the future. We cry out, "Help! Is anybody there?" Oh, that alone feeling is debilitating! "Ahhhhh!" "Give me instant comfort! And there isn't any. Not until we have figured out how to create it from within. Not in an esoteric way like a guru or anything like that, but within our own brain and body. After all, isn't that where it really matters? They are our own brains and bodies. Shouldn't we be in charge of them?

So, how do we get there? That is the question that has plagued humankind for thousands of years. A part of the problem is that we have forgotten what we want or don't think it is possible to get it. So many of us are just getting by or are just trying to get by. If we are in this state, no wonder we have anxiety, depression, or anger problems.

I have been helping thousands of people understand how their history affects their ability to live in the present. I was once told to ask myself "What do I want?" It took some time to answer. Why? I had been following what I believed to be true for a long time and it was just not working. I had to understand that my understanding of reality was skewed and that I had to make some adjustments. My main problem was that if my reality was off, how would I know what reality was and how could I alter that reality? I did not know what to do!! I could not believe that *all* of the old stuff I understood was in error. So, how was I to proceed into changing my reality? This felt incredibly unsafe.

What is important to note here is that we can become aware of our patterns of the past that have become firmly set, and we can change their effect on us by changing our behavior. Unfortunately, this only affects what we are aware of. Worse yet, we can't always change our behavior because some old patterns are too strong. There are those that would say awareness can be influenced by positive input through deep relaxation and in a calm quiet state. In a relaxed state, the mind is not cluttered with a mixture of thoughts. Then, learning can take pace with clarity. Also, during relaxation, a calm sense of being with yourself can allow a sensation of accomplishment. In other words, you can cease fighting and struggling as you become clearer. Relaxation can enable you to approach a situation with a greater feeling of confidence.

Not every relaxation is aimed at adding positive input to awareness. Some are meant to create awareness of feelings and emotions. While relaxing, you are directed at the discovery of your own resources in order to change a situation. You can, with learning, change simply through your intention or self-suggestion. Until new awareness is reached, the old patterns of behavior have the tendency to continue and can even have the feeling of being out of control.

Essentially, through relaxing, you can learn how to change your own neural pathways in a new direction that allows you to reach your goals. The problem is there are quite a few variables blocking this path. Neural pathways which drive involuntary behaviors may not be comfortable with efforts to be or remain calm. If this is true, they flood the consciousness with fight and flight signals which are quite intrusive and may be accompanied by physical sensations such as twitching, jittery feelings, shortness of breath, nausea, and possibly others.

The best example is like when planting seeds. We certainly have the desire and the intention that the seeds and the plants will grow. However, there are many factors out of our immediate control that will affect that outcome. We can do everything correctly; plant the seeds, water them, and yet, they do not grow. Our firmly planted intentions and desires may require assistance to bear fruit. Just like planting seeds, we can strengthen the possibilities by following the advice of experienced farmers and gardeners.

One of the first things I had to do to change was institute the "DFM" principle in my life. Earlier I explained that I used this to thwart my involuntary nervous system's fight and flight messages to me and that I applied the "first thought wrong" principle. When I described this earlier, it was to just survive. Now I want to change. Accordingly, I had to alter the use of DFM a bit.

I spoke earlier about the differentiation of needs, wants and desires. As I began planting the seeds of change in myself, I spent some time differentiating my needs from my wants and desires. So, as thoughts would come in my head, I shifted the DFM to "Does it Fundamentally Matter". In other words, is this a need? If I could honestly say that I would die if I did not follow the message from my involuntary nervous system, I decided it was a need. Otherwise, I applied the original DFM. (Doesn't F*cking Matter). This began my journey of analyzing and understanding our animal instincts.

I have found that "DFMing" our animal instincts allows us to live from a higher level of humanity. Due to my work with the neurofeedback of thousands of people, I realized that the classic forms of neurofeedback may actually work to re-institute animal instincts. Most Neurofeedback systems that I am aware of guide people's neural activity via a normative database which contains a high level of animal instinctual patterning. This patterning is exactly what I had been spending so much time DFMing. This is why I created the protocol for Neurofeedforward. Through Neurofeedforward, I help people create neural pathways that differ from the ones their system has been creating in their past.

We can also plant our intentions firmly in our hearts. We can tell ourselves, "This is what I really want," over and over. Then, since our nervous system develops based on habitual patterns and repetition, we may feel our intentions as they grow in our minds, neural pathways, and in our behaviors. It is a matter of cause and effect. The same can be true, over time with good conditioning, for our thoughts, emotions and behaviors. If you plant and nurture loving thoughts you can reap loving emotions.

The above descriptions of Biofeedback and Neurofeedback show that these systems work to help people change. The descriptions also provide the reasons why I created NeuroEmpowerment and technology to help in a very different way, a much more highly effective and longer lasting way.

Ask Yourself "What Do I Want?"

That brings us to the biggest question of all: What do YOU want? If you don't know, or you are feeling somewhat confused, allow yourself ten or fifteen minutes of silence and solitude. Take a break! It will be well worth it!

Now, ask the same question over and over. "What do I want, and what do I really, really want?" Then wait, just wait. You will be listening to what is coming from inside yourself based on what you really want. Other thoughts come in that you don't want. Just go back to the question, over and over, and just that one question. You will come to focusing on the question, then listening, then focusing on the answer. If it's not entirely clear, that's ok. The answers may start popping in later in the day. "Aha", you will say, "Ah yes, that's what I really want."

It's like you are learning how to inspire yourself! Then, as you are going to sleep tonight, ask again and again, "What did I say I want?" The answers will keep coming as long as you keep asking in silence and in solitude. Wait and listen. That's something new in the multi-tasking craziness of today, isn't it?

Do this over and over each day. This simple exercise can cause a new focus. The focus that you want. You are even creating the beginning of getting what you want. You can plant those seeds!

Back to the question, "What do I really want", your mind (and body) creates and opens the door to the possibility and creates the direction of reaching your desired goal. Write it down as if it is going to happen. Pay attention to how you feel about it in your mind and body. Bodily sensations can be a good indicator of how our unconscious (involuntary survival based nervous system) feels about what we are thinking about.

Okay, now I am going to answer the question for you. Here is the answer => *You want to be happy*. Whatever you were thinking you wanted is your perception of what will make you happy. Interestingly enough, I have people say, "I just want to be satisfied". First of all, I think that is kind of sad. Why not strive for happiness? If you are making goals and desires for your future, why aim so low? Is it out of fear?

The reality is that if you just want to be satisfied, that is what will make you happy in the context that I mean it here. Resistance to "being happy" is often tied up with negative experiences with happiness in our past. It often feels like it is easier to be sad, angry or miserable than it is to be happy. The negative actually seems easier to control. This is another reason many people choose to be "not happy".

You Can Transform

This discussion of "happiness" brings us back to needs, wants and likes. Needs are what are necessary for survival. Wants and likes are those things that you think will make you happy. Any limitations are only a part of your old thinking— fear-based thinking. I call it your old "stinkin thinkin!" Now you get into the fun and very creative part of your new process. Let's call it holding on to what you want and letting go of what didn't work in the past to exist as the real YOU. With the real you comes many awesome feelings. The feeling of

- being in control of yourself,
- of knowing how you think, how you respond to your environment and its influence, and
- of how to stay on track toward your goals and carry them to completion

You now have your own private secret to success. You have all the resources you need within yourself. When you know yourself better and understand and accept how you got to be the way you are, you can clear out the past and go forward. Enjoy the success each day as you come closer to your desired outcomes. If you slip backwards, take a moment or two to ask yourself what is happening. "Am I living from fear or love?" The path of love takes you to the real you.

If you are not going in the direction you want, change the direction! You are the choice maker! So much of what we do is our choice! If we do not like the outcomes of our past choices, we CAN change our choices. It may come with some pain, but it is our choice whether to suffer or not. Changing direction and making new choices in the feeling, function, and behavior department are simple, however, they are definitely not easy!

If or when we realize that we want to change a feeling, function, or behavior, we have to counteract all the neural pathways that contain past repetitions of those feelings, functions or behaviors. Accordingly, this will require creating energy that is intentionally void of past feelings, functions, or behaviors. Instead, we must create new ones that are energized with the desired feelings, functions, or behaviors.

This will require many choices and redirections. We have to keep making the decision to change the old and bring in the new. Depending on what kind of feeling, function, or behavior it is, this can take three weeks to three years of repetition for the new to be strong enough to become the new normal. The times and depth of entrainment can be enhanced and speed up through neurofeedback, NeuroEmpowerment and Neurofeedforward.

We have been given the ability to transform. I have never seen anything give a person as much energy as a vision that he or she is developing to bring into reality. I have seen people forsake sleep, food, and comfort for the sake of a project that they love. I can remember that when I had a vision of being my ideal self and realized the possibility, I was unstoppable.

There is something very magical about a person dedicated to a purpose, something more precious than I can attempt to put into words. It is what carried me when I was in jail and my children were kept from me by the court system. It is the miracle of creation. It is exactly this miracle which enables us to transcend circumstances. This is the same energy that moved the Einsteins and the Edisons to change the world. This is the same energy that helped Nelson Mandela survive his incarceration.

We have an inspiration, a thought, inside ourselves that draws us to our own excellence, if we are willing to listen and act on it. Within you lie talents far greater than you have recognized and expressed, and it is your imagination that causes you to trigger a possibility. Whatever you can imagine is possible for you to create, and when you imagine yourself as you desire, as if it has already become a reality, you are giving a signal to your own internal self (mentally and physically) that you are ready to be who you want to be.

When you see yourself in your imagination, this not only causes you to think about your possibilities, but you realize you are capable of becoming your desired self. It is the simple law of cause and effect. Imagination is literally the workshop of the mind. If you think about it, all your ideas of what you want to have been fashioned in your mind and your body (as described above). Many of your limitations may no longer exist.

Many of us cannot figure it out completely ahead of time. We may just know that we do not like certain ways we feel or behave. This is where I had to start. So, do not worry if you cannot imagine the "you" that you want to be. Maybe you can identify just one trait, characteristic, feeling, function of behavior you want to change and then work on that. Then you can move onto the next characteristic and so on. That is what I had to do. It still works exactly as described above.

I cannot tell you (because it happened multiple times along the way) how many times I was doing great and then hit another deep low. Was it back to the drawing table: "Oh no! Does that mean starting from scratch?" Often, if I sat with my feelings for a while, I could tell that the feelings were not as bad as they used to be. It is so important to remember at these times that it is about progress and not perfection.

There does not seem to be a "nirvana plateau" that I was able to reach and then everything was perfect from then on. Life, with all of its hardships and high moments, continues on. So, when in doubt of my progress, I would sit quietly with my eyes closed and think of my life as a timeline. I would then look back at my past and all my internal identity and functional problems. I would "see" how far I had come and focus on gratitude for that. I would then turn and look forward down the timeline and feel how it was going to be if I kept at it and kept progressing. By doing this exercise, I was reminded that this is a process that takes time. A process that required nurturing and loving myself.

I wish it was as easy as flipping some switches, but it is not. Why is it so hard? One reason is that when we were growing up, (even among our friends sometimes) our schools to our jobs (for some - jail or prison), the media, and social media are told who to be. Think about it. How many times have we gotten the message "you need to do _____ in order to be _____". These blanks were filled with things to do for home, school, or work to be what those at home school or work wanted you to be. We learned that "boys don't cry and that they should always be strong" not "boys should know themselves and be true to themselves". There are obviously hundreds of these types of beliefs that have been instilled in us that do not serve us at all. These beliefs are often called "limiting beliefs".

I have helped thousands continue to develop through NeuroEmpowerment. I have seen thousands of people bring an end to their suffering and open up to and live exciting new possibilities and lives. I have found that at the core of what most often needs to change in order for us to transform is the concept of safety. It may seem obvious, but I am going to say it anyway. The reason or cause of most, if not all, of our survival instincts is this deep underlying idea that we are not safe.

There are many detrimental elements of our animal instincts that no longer serve many humans which are causing more trouble than good. These instincts may have been very important for all humans tens of thousands of years ago and are still important to some humans now. One of these concepts is that we are not safe. This intrinsic belief gets compounded by another animal instinct of "finding what is wrong" which creates a more complicated fear that being safe is the most dangerous state of being.

This is one of the most detrimental instincts. The neurological belief that "we are not safe when we are safe". It is caused by a common in utero experience. In the last trimester of pregnancy, we are just discovering ourselves, our fingers, etc. and starting to form core neural pathways which contain original information regarding our understanding of who we are. We are in a wonderful place, the belly of our mother, and we may feel safe until mom feels a wave of anxiety.

That wave interferes with the setting in the womb disrupting our "safe" feeling environment. After this happens a few times, many of us (as fetuses) get very active on an ongoing basis, presumably to create our own chaos so that when the chaos of a cortisol (an anxiety hormone) wave hits we feel more in control. This is easily recognizable in people when sitting in a room because they cannot sit still. They feel as if they have to shake a leg, wiggle their fingers, shift in their chairs etc. Their nervous system is trying to create continual movement because they learned in the womb that constant action helps make them feel safe. Unfortunately, we are safest when we have nothing left to lose, which basically means when we are dead. I believe that this is why so many people are moved toward suicide by the unconscious levels of the mind.

I have developed a formula regarding "safety" that works in my wellness center and worked in jail. I utilize this "safety formula" in our center and will use it to help the world change from functioning from the tribal frameworks which are "fear" driven to a framework of functioning from love of self and love of others.

You Are Not The Slave Of Your Nervous System

I have been very surprised at the stories that people tell me and that the inmates told. Many justified their actions of stealing, burglarizing, and harming others, explaining they were victims, defending themselves, their territory or even their right to live. Most people justify how they are feeling and functioning as if they have no choice in the matter. I hear people saying things that describe themselves or their feelings or functions as if they were and are separate personae. They say things like, I was an only child, I have A.D.D. etc.

Our society has taught us to give away our internal power by defining, judging, and labeling patterns of living as if we have no power over them. I feel as if they are half-way correct. It is definitely true if we believe it's true.

I feel truly blessed that I have been through so much trouble and for my incarceration. Through my experiences, I have been provided an amazing opportunity to learn so much. Many people do not get to learn the lessons that I have. In jail, many of my cellmates were living in the same five block radius that their parents and grandparents had. They clearly were not given much opportunity to advance out of that circumstance. They also were not taught right from wrong the same way I and so many people are.

Many of the people I have treated in the clinic also have not had the teaching experiences to allow them to learn what I have. All of our choices and opportunities have been limited. Very few speak about how they could have done it better, and how they would do it better. A lot of that was because they had no idea of a better way. Their survival instincts push them to do as the tribe does. Everyone they knew did it the way they did it, which makes it "right".

In the therapeutic process, it is important for the patient to be provided a different perspective which can make it easier to see and process their mistakes. In my process I provide a different perspective for people to understand how they behaved in the past. This allows them to dismiss all shame about the past in order to be able to use the past as a guide for how to act now. A part of the "how to act" now is to keep in mind all of the future "nows" when conditioning the nervous system to perform the way they want.

Many people have had significant fear of the future which was developed by their past. I have helped people to experience a new awareness, even new awakenings. It is often important to seek advice from others when trying to imagine a better life. Many people often pontificate about how it might have been if they had known better, and had they not made the mistakes they were now so dearly paying for.

Through our perspective that events condition the function of the nervous system and that "conditioning" can be influenced and redirected to serve us, they were able to make meaningful change rapidly.

The fear-based pack animal survival mechanisms are present for all humans at some point in their lives. Most people are living with these mechanisms as defining factors for their lives. I have found this to be true with my most wealthy and famous clients as well as with my less fortunate and young clients. I also found this to be true with the men I met while incarcerated. Many of them were more worried about surviving in their neighborhoods than they were about surviving in jail.

Small glimpses of courage sometimes began to echo in the cells. And why? Perhaps because of the desire to be free. Perhaps because of the desire to have another chance. At first, they didn't seem to feel worthy of having another chance. In some cases, they harmed others and their guilt and shame added to their feeling broken. Many were broken, stuck, and searching for another way.

The hard part of this segment of their journey is that it had to begin with a cry for help. They needed a beginning of showing their vulnerability, of being real, of facing themselves, even letting go of all the anger, and blame. I began to teach this to some of them. It was difficult because it almost meant seeking a new reality, like leaving earth. This is exactly what they had to do, leave the small part of earth they knew. They had to "see" an alternative.

I began to provide a small description, which acted like a window, of a different way to live their lives by describing my life and teaching them a few tools and techniques to think differently. They were able to relate with many aspects of my life which helped them decide to make some small changes to move in the same direction as my life. When this happened, I taught them tools and techniques to assist them in conditioning their nervous systems to change.

Hitting rock bottom can be the trigger for a new awakening. Pain may be one of the greatest motivators. Pain is not necessary though. Pain can also be a blocker, or more specifically, fear of pain. Pain in the form of shame, blame, anger, and guilt often blocks us from being real. Talking about it in a group of others who completely understood helped to ease the pain and lessen the misery.

When one can say, "I am not alone", it can often help the pain seem less horrifying. This may be a "good" use of the pack animal mechanism. Often, when someone becomes vulnerable, they also become loveable. My cell mates may have become sorry for their mistakes, but they found out they were not just their mistakes! They were much more. Their behaviors were a result of being real human beings caught up in a shaming "not being worthy" culture. They were fearful of others being better than them, which in the pack animal framework meant that they were not safe.

Many were kept in an environment that inhibited their ability to grow and learn. Often people's own pack-animal mentality causes them to get "stuck" in and perpetuate living conditions and belief systems generation to generation which are detrimental to them. Perhaps they are "failures" in their own minds because they were "not good enough, not smart enough, or their parents didn't care enough". The reality is, they were not given much of a chance to "succeed."

I realized that a lot of their anger came from constantly being told or shown that they were "less than" and somewhere deep inside, they knew it was a lie. They knew they were worthy of being equal to or even better than, yet they were not aware of how that could possibly be true. Everything in their reality "proved" that it was not true. So, of course, they are angry. I began to help them see the reality that everyone is worthy and good enough just because they are breathing. I helped them see that they had the power to be whatever kind of person they wanted to be.

I helped many men see that they were behaving as victims because they were victims. It is extremely confusing. However, thinking like a victim causes people to be victims even when they do not have to be. Many people do not see themselves as victims and at the same time do not know how to live in another way which perpetuates them being victims. I helped them see that they were acting perfectly human. They were living life based on how the world (the 5-block neighborhood and their parents) had taught them. I helped them see that it was not their fault, however, if they kept behaving the same way, then it was their fault. I helped them see that their behavior was the behavior of victims of their circumstances. I helped them see that they could and that it was time to start thinking in a different way.

The next step was to help them see that no one is better than anyone else. I explained that we are all human. Humans are fear-based pack animals. As I said earlier in this book, they call our packs, "tribes". I helped them see that tribes create the tiers of "better than" as part of the fear-based culture and our society was just one big tribe made up of many other tribes. I helped them understand that it seemed like their tribe (the people in the five block neighborhood) was necessary to survive, but that living in "their hoods" was actually trapping them, and since there were lots of other tribes around (including the police force) that were constantly enacting "tribal warfare" on them, continuing the tribal framework for living actually made survival less possible.

As is true for most of us, the tribe we are born into is necessary for our survival, however, once we become adults, this society gives lots of options which make the "tribe" no longer critical for survival. My experience has shown that this is true for most of us. There are tribes available for the executives, for the executives' spouses, for the athletes, the service personnel, the factory workers, the government workers, the students, the parents, the teachers, etc. There are "tribes" available for all demographics in our society.

I have literally helped thousands of people make meaningful change in their lives. It has become a natural part of my life. Even in jail, I was helping people. There was one man in jail in particular that quickly began to listen to me and decided to change his ways. As I mentioned in my personal story, his name was Terril Lomax, but he introduced himself as and others called him "Wolf". He was 40 years old when we met. He had 15 children and barely knew any of them. He had spent 19 of his 40 years in and out of jail and prison.

He opened up to me, and we examined the error of his ways. He was very angry, because he thought that was a normal way to live life. As I discussed earlier, many people in his situation are angry. As with many people in society, his role models and mentors were all angry.

When our mentors and role models live from fear and harbor various levels of anger, it seems normal for us to carry resentments and anger from our past in our daily lives. So, living life angry is "normal" for many people and was "normal" for him. I have witnessed this with many of our Supermind clients. This is also a characteristic that caused me to stop interacting with some of my past mentors.

Through my many years of experience, I have come to understand that anger is a waste of time. We get angry when something that has already happened (most of the time) that we think is not as it should be or as we want it to be. If it happened, it is what it is. Our anger is just our opinion regarding what happened. Since it did happen, our opinion is obviously not accurate. I have learned that the more quickly we move into acceptance and forgiveness and then see what we can do to change what is happening or may happen in the future without anger, the better the outcomes. Some people say that anger is a great motivator. I have come to learn that love is a much better motivator than anger.

I teach people and taught Wolf how to let go of their anger and replace it with love and create joy from within through meditation. I teach a breathing technique accompanied by imagining that one is in a calm, quiet, safe and happy place. I also help people realize that most of the time when they are meditating, they already are in a safe, calm, quiet place. Many people have a hard time with that, because they have few memories of those kinds of places. This was particularly true for Wolf. He had grown up in the inner city where life was more about survival than enjoyment. I taught him, as I have taught so many others, how to create that inside of him.

It is easy for us to get our understanding of how to live life all wrong. Human survival instincts are anchored in the tribal mentality. Most of our societal frameworks maintain and often escalate the tribal mechanisms. It is natural for humans to build our organizations and governments and deal with others under this framework. It is much easier to govern a flock or a herd than it is to govern free thinking and free people.

Within the societal framework, different segments are part of the "system" and therefore, the system has built in protocol to keep the segments as they are so the system can live on. This is natural, not some "conspiracy theory." Most of the tribal behavioral patterns and systems were and are built in order to help us get safe when we already are safe. This is why they are no longer needed.

With Wolf, I went on to tell him "You are really missing out on one of the greatest experiences in life, raising and being a good father to children. We decided together that he "needed" to get out of jail, get a job, show the courts he really meant to be straight and be a good father so he could get his children back (they had been wards of the state before living with his brother).

With many people, I help them to correct their misunderstandings and choose a different way to live their lives. As I did with Wolf, I help them understand that there is nothing wrong with them, just something wrong with how they had been behaving and living their lives. So, when they can learn to love themselves as they are and begin to live their lives differently, their lives get dramatically better.

That is exactly what I have seen so many people do and what Wolf did. For nine years (until his death in 2022), he fathered those children as a single father and stayed straight. He was a law-abiding member of society, a good father, a good son, a good brother, a good friend, a car owner, and a home owner until his death. The road was not easy, but he was true to himself and his children. He used meditation as the bedrock of his strength. When he learned there was nothing wrong with him, it became easier for him to call me and ask for help. I was able to guide him through stressful situations and keep moving forward.

It is amazing what happens in families, workplaces, and other groups when people start to live from a place of truth. My jail experience was a great microcosm for what happens to societies when the misunderstandings are corrected and consciousness shifts. As I described earlier, in jail the cellmates became less defensive, and stopped hurting or even having the idea of hurting each other. It all started with the idea that "I am safe" and "there is nothing wrong with me. There is something wrong with my situation and the way I have been behaving."

In other words, they began to love themselves so they could love (or be kind to) others. They began to confide in each other, and with that arrived the sense of connection, the sense of belonging to each other with care instead of violence. With belonging instead of defensiveness. They were not weaker from sharing with each other, they were stronger (this is counterintuitive for the animal instinctual part of us). They found new courage to allow their dreams and desires to come back into their lives. I saw what worked in jail work for families and workplaces. I believe it will work in the world around us. I have developed a formula to facilitate changing the population of the world from this and my many other experiences.

I witnessed and learned that vulnerability allows not only a cry for help, but an acknowledgement of each person that they are not bad people. Their lives are not over. Rather there is a window of ability due to the allowing of sharing, caring, and understanding of themselves and others better. By connecting with themselves and others, people experience a new way of living. The connection causes an awakening. The connection causes a feeling of relief, not profound, but a start of acknowledging new possibilities. Yes, being sorry for the past is different than shame for being a failed person. It means that there is a road forward learning from the past rather than being trapped in it with no way out. Hope restores us with new desires and goals to advance new awakenings.

The old critical voice can stay active even though it does silence a bit as we gain understanding from others, connect and relate. We realize that we are all just trying to do the best we can as fellow imperfect humans on this journey of life. We have learned that by changing the mind we are able to change behavior. It can bring about the feeling of being able to survive and not stay broken down. It can be like a new breath of fresh air, a new breath of life itself. In the solitude and silence of their cells, there came a renewal, in a sense, of how things could be.

It is because of this experience and so many others in my lifetime and what I have witnessed in others that I hesitate to judge things as "good" or "bad". What seems good often turns out to be bad and vice versa. It reminds me of that old story of the man in the village who obtains a new stallion. The village people say to the man "How great it is that you have a new stallion." The man replies, "it just is." That week his son fell off the horse and broke his leg. The village people said, "Oh, how horrible, your son fell and broke his leg." The man just said, "It is what it is". The next week the emperor's men came to the village and took all the sons and young men that could fight to be part of the emperor's armies. His son was excluded because of his broken leg. The village people were thrilled. The story could go on and on. My life experiences have similarly shown me that what may seem good often can turn bad and vice versa.

All psychological change is coupled with physiological change and vice-versa. Every thought and emotion is recorded in our body. Change can be difficult in the beginning because of all of our thoughts that have become habitual ways of thinking. We have unwittingly gone down the path of anxiety because we didn't know how to not have anxiety. In other words, we hadn't learned how to get rid of fear and follow the process of rejuvenation both in our minds and in our bodies at the same time. So, not only do we not know how, but we also lack the physiology to make it happen. This means that we actually lack the neural pathways linked to the twelve systems of the body (and more) in order to make it happen.

It takes time and practice to build the necessary neural pathways. Due to the fact that most of the connections happen while sleeping, the practice has to be performed over multiple days so that our sleep process can connect the change with the 12 systems of the body. All 12 systems are not connected in one night. It takes multiple days to make these connections. It takes even longer to strengthen them sufficiently enough to replace the older patterns in the involuntary nervous system.

Belief systems play a critical role in guiding our neuron creation (Neurogenesis), neurons are the nerve cells which make up our nerves which leads to neural pathway creation, strengthening, and use. Every neuronal channel, when the neuron is created, is created because our system believes that it is needed. Belief systems therefore exist at all levels of our psyche and neurological anatomy.

True control of neurological responses and function rely on our ability to transcend or fully harness our nature as humans. Our survival instincts as fear-based pack animals cause our involuntary nervous systems to constantly push us into tribal behavior. These instincts naturally provide the guidance for the nerves which are sensing our environment and sending the signals to the other parts of us. The content and strength of those signals vary based on our perceptions and exposure to what it is that we are sensing.

What this means is that our beliefs are a main part of harnessing our nature as humans. Through the process of retraining our brains, we can face fear head on and change our neural pathway responses to function in line with how and who we want to be at 10 to 100 times the speed that we can do it on our own.

Our Tribal Instincts Rob Us Of Our "Power"

As our survival instincts drive us to be and stay a part of a tribe, any tribe, they focus our attention on becoming and being the person, the tribe wants us to be. Societies across the globe are extremely practiced at robbing the power of individuals "for the greater good"! It is an overstepping of the fantastic slogan "All for one and one for all!"

There have been and continue to be times when this was necessary for the survival of the individuals and the societies they are part of. Unfortunately, due to nervous system function and lack of awareness of the best use of these ideas for the benefits "of all", a high percentage of populations have confused identities. A big part of this confusion directly affects people's personal power.

In western societies there is a widespread message that alone you are powerless and that true power is gained by mass. The message seems to be something like "The more people who act and behave the way you do, the safer you are. Forget how you feel and want to function, act the way we show you and model for you. If something stops you from this, then we can give you a pill or find some other external mechanism to change you. That is correct, we can change you so you can be more acceptable to us." This is clearly not the explicit message. I am not aware that anyone is actually saying that message in that way. It is just an underlying theme.

Around 2010, the demographic with the highest increase in psychologically based medications were people under two years of age. The babies were just not acting "good" enough for the families (tribe), so they were medicating their babies so they would act better. Soothing, which leads the way to self-soothing, was just thrown out the window. The message "you can't so we will" became a trend of medicating babies. This inhibited those babies from being able to develop the coping and self-regulation skills which are part of psychological well-being. It robbed them of their power and taught them not to develop the power of self-control.

This same dynamic is also true regarding our ability to self-regulate and be self-reliant. It is extremely tempting to turn to getting help or quick solutions rather than developing determination or internal skills of processing life on a daily basis and life's challenging moments. For example, many people learn early in life to "take a pill or powder" for a headache instead of drinking some water, breathing, or relaxing.

How often have we heard someone say, "I need a drink", meaning they want to imbibe some alcohol in order to relax instead of just breathing and relaxing. Medical experts say that many of the most common medical conditions (some terminal) are avoidable. Common behaviors of our societies have fostered these conditions to reach the levels they have attained.

This may be true for our immune systems. It seems to be common practice to quickly take antibiotics if we are feeling sick rather than working through the illness. There are many people that are getting vaccines to avoid flus and other non-life-threatening maladies seemingly just to avoid the inconvenience of having to fight through a cold.

I am not saying that antibiotics and vaccines are bad. I am saying that we cannot be vaccinated for everything and if we turn to antibiotics every time we feel sick, how can we possibly develop our immune system to fight through colds and viruses? I am for the appropriate use of vaccines and antibiotics (one that keeps us safe and allows for the strengthening of our immune systems).

Many people have proven that we humans are powerful. I am saying let's spend more time teaching people to develop their internal abilities rather than to go buy something to do that for them. The saying "teach a man to fish rather than just give him fish" comes to mind. The practice of teaching people to find and nurture their true selves got lost in the idea of the greater good.

The fact of the matter is that most societies will do just fine if they stop trying to require the members of their societies to give up their personal identities in order to conform with their communal identity. I believe that it is a better formula to communicate the values of the society and encourage people with values that align with the values of the community to join and nurture the community. In this way, the community will in turn nurture those values for the individual.

The dynamic of our survival being dependent on "All for one, and one for all" has passed. Our individual and racial survival is no longer dependent on tribal mechanisms. This is mainly true because the tribal mechanisms are widespread, extremely diverse, and easily accessible.

It is important to note that I am speaking about being able to live anxiety free, which requires an understanding of the difference between needs, wants, and likes, as described earlier. My statements are only true because the world has become extremely developed and is composed of many strong functional societies. We can now shift from their (societies) survival and our individual survival being mutually important. For the most part, no matter what an individual does, the existence of today's societies is not threatened.

Accordingly, it is time for us (humans) to understand how to get our needs met through the widespread resources available and then focus on becoming the best person we can be, according to us. It is time for us to be in charge of our moods without needing a drink or drug to alter our moods for us. It is time for us all to find out who we are and in what way we enjoy being most powerful and nurture that power. This brings us back to the importance of inner peace and personal power.

Finding Your Inner Peace and Personal Power

Living a life free from anxiety, and having inner peace, is often difficult to achieve because our natural animal instincts drive us to constantly assess, interact with, and be affected by our environment. We often try to find peace by creating a peaceful outer environment. For example, sitting in a comfortable chair in a comfortable position and playing peaceful music.

Many times, we will also further give away our power by taking a substance to create inner peace while we are in this space listening to this music. Finding and creating your inner peace enhances your inner power.

We are powerful beings with the ability to create. I found that it was vitally important to be able to create a real and powerful calm and enjoyable space inside of me that would help every level of my being fully appreciate that "I am" actually very safe and can enjoy what is happening "now" from the inside out.

With this power, what was happening around me no longer could dictate how I felt. I was able to be fully present from my "inner peaceful place", survey the environment from love of myself and others rather than from fear of what was and might happen to me, and see how I could help those around me rather than just protect myself or show up as the best in the room.

I began by trying to meditate. I failed. My regrets, remorse, and resentment would not let me sit still long enough or self-direct my thinking and/or my feelings. After I practiced for a while, I got a second or two of peace. Then I was able to expand that second or two into five or 10 seconds. My ability to create peace in my mind kept expanding until I could do it for hours. This took years of work and practice.

Finding peace was important for me because I was going through an extreme amount of trauma and could not find any peace. The trauma I was going through was not in just one area of my life. I was learning to meditate and create inner peace during the time when my traumas included:

- My father dying in my arms
- My wife leaving me
- My assets being frozen and liquidated
- Having to move out of and sell my house
- Loses of my business
- Loss of my career
- Dealing with the 32 lawsuits against me
- Being indicted for fraud, racketeering and a few other things
- I was "shamed" publicly
- I lost many friends
- I was under investigation by various government entities
- Worst of all, I lost 65% custody of my children

Needless to say, those five seconds of peace I was able to get were *AMAZING* and vitally important for my sanity. I had to learn how to meditate just so I could get some sleep. This is exactly what I did. I began to get more and more moments of peace. I take meditation to another level. Through years of practice, I have become very proficient at meditation. I use it to entrain my involuntary nervous system to function more like I want it to rather than just follow my animal and/or survival instincts.

When I began learning how to meditate and attended meditation events, I was and am told things like; "Begin your relaxation and quiet time with yourself by choosing a position. Sit in your chair with an aware but comfortable posture, your back straight, hands resting in your lap and your feet flat on the floor. Loosen any tight clothing like belts and shoes and just notice the objects that surround you whether in your home or out in nature. Notice the stillness of your body. Begin to notice your breathing, just notice. Take a minute or two to notice the rhythm of your breathing as your stomach and chest rises and falls with every breath naturally and without effort. Breathe in and just notice as the air begins to flow from your nose down into your shoulders and into your stomach. A sense of ease and easiness begins to flow into your whole body and you are totally aware of that happening."

When I started, this was not possible nor desirable. Now it happens almost naturally. Except, I do not have to control my position or my surroundings anymore. Now I can meditate while walking, riding a bike, or at an event.

So, let's get back to how you can become more aware of, entrain, condition, nurture, love and develop different levels of your consciousness in order to create a sustainable stable inner peace. When many people say oh, you mean meditate?! I say, yes and no. Meditation is typically a process (and there are many types of meditation) in which the practitioners or the meditators themselves are guiding you (or themselves) into a certain "state of being" or interacting differently (stopping the "chatter" or racing thoughts etc.) with the levels of consciousness and their internal "parts". Most meditations are about the "now". Which means separating from regrets, remorse, or resentments from the past and worries about the future.

The "finding your inner peace" practice includes going beyond the "now". It is meditation, plus redirecting, reprogramming, practicing, and actuating peace. In my work, I have been able to identify neurological patterns which create peace. This is helpful by providing a target pattern to set the neurofeedback mechanisms to and to confirm how well a person is finding peace. Through this process people create new neural pathways and neural networks which contain their inner peace. The more they access and strengthen the "inner peace" neural networks, the more present "inner peace" becomes in their daily lives. It becomes a base part of them that they can access at will and enjoy.

It is perfectly natural for our unconscious and subconscious mind through sensory neural pathways to want us to worry about the future or think about the past or to have the mind wander. Some thoughts might be distressing, which often makes meditation seem very difficult or even impossible. Often the instruction from a meditation guide is that when you have distressing thoughts to simply notice them without judgment. I have heard them say "If a negative thought or feeling grabs your attention then, just notice it and then return to focusing on your breath." In the beginning, I found this impossible or nearly impossible. Of course, I was not sure what "judgment" meant at the time. It's natural for your mind to wander. In our society, it is also somewhat natural for us to be critical of ourselves. This does not mean that it is good for us. It certainly is not pleasant and helpful in us being able to be happy.

I had a meditation guide say once, "Regarding negative or critical thinking of ourselves, recognize that it is simply a thought. It is what your mind does. You can notice it and then let it go." I have since learned not to do that. Especially since I learned that our thoughts are on neural pathways which are parts of our bodies and are becoming "permanent" parts of us. I now say, "Do not ever allow yourself to be mean to you. Be your own best friend!"

It may help to imagine and picture yourself in a loving place you like to be or have liked to be in the past either with others or by yourself. Help your thoughts flow like the wind or like a beautiful sound of music that you love.

Self-Betterment Exercises

Since meditation is usually for the "now" and can be a double edge sword I do not like to use meditation alone in the practice of making change within ourselves. As I said earlier, I go beyond just meditating. I practice entraining my body to think for me. Accordingly, when teaching how to enact change through mindfulness techniques, I call the practice "Self-Betterment Exercises" (SBEs). This is a form of meditation where the intent is to know ourselves in the now (and our past) and then entrain our nervous system to function differently for the future "nows".

In each moment, how you feel is just an energy pattern. It is just a specific collection of neural pathways firing in an appropriate sequence within our bodies in order to create this feeling. If we practice enough SBEs, we can recreate pretty much any of the patterns that we practice whenever we want to. In this way, we can practice dealing with difficult people or situations in our lives differently in order to handle being with them in the future without being as affected.

You can make a decision to take action in the direction you want. To make this decision is to direct your thoughts and desires directly into action. It's the case for all of us, if we flounder in indecision and procrastination, we can lose our power. If you make mistakes along the way, make a decision to accept them and forgive yourself. Remember, always be your own best friend. You have the power for sure!

Each morning, I formulate a plan of taking three steps in my desire or toward creating what I want while saying, "I can do this, and I will". Three steps are possible today, and that's enough. This helps me not to get overwhelmed. The reality is that I typically take more than just 3 steps. So, this practice helps me feel good about myself because I am doing more than I expected of myself.

Staying in this day with your three steps can keep you in the present without flip flopping into the past or even the future. Stay present on this day. Stay with your three steps only and you can stay in focus. Every decision takes courage, because we face the unknown. No longer can those old habits have a hold on us, so we take a leap of courage to even take the first step. You are being courageous enough to direct your life. You deserve the best of all that you already are. That is really what NeuroEmpowerment is all about, being the best version of ourselves each and every day.

My passion is to teach others how to be more of who they want to be. I help them to figure out and step into being the best version of themselves. That "best version" is based on their opinion, not mine. To help people do this, I often share my journey and the process I took and take to getting to the state of mind that I enjoy most. The first step in this process is figuring out what that "best version" of us looks like. It is of course forever evolving.

Journaling is one of two methods you can use in order to figure out "the best version of yourself". The other is finding a person who is not emotionally involved with you, and whom you are not emotionally attached to, to act as an advisor. The absence of emotional involvement allows for objectivity. Once you have that person, you want to share your beliefs on how well you are doing, and what you think is the best version of yourself. They can advise you as to how healthy the version sounds and be unabashedly honest and direct with you.

Enjoying living is much easier when we can understand what that "best version" is based on. When I know that I am performing at my highest, I feel the best I can in every way. That feeling gives more energy than anything, and it is a feeling of pleasure about who I am. How can it get any better than that?

I started this journaling and sharing with an advisor practice in 1995 and continue it to this day. It is important to journal in a way that helps to continually define (loosely) and evolve the beliefs of what the "best version of you" is. In this way we have meaningful information to share with our advisor.

When I started the journaling process, I went through many different ways of journaling. The process of journaling I am referring to here is meant to provide a formula to reach higher levels of fulfillment and joy. It begins with writing down our roles. For example, I am a husband, an ex-husband, a father, a son, a brother etc. I then wrote out what I believed my best version of those roles could be. Today, when I journal, I write out how well I fill those roles according to what fulfills me and makes me happy. I then sit with my trusted advisor to review my journaling and adjust my perceptions as necessary so I can continue to grow in the direction I would like.

I ended up running into some trouble by following this formula. I had forgotten a very important role which was the role of taking care of myself first so I could then fulfill the other roles. I found myself "losing myself" in a mire of too much service to others. As I said earlier, I enjoy helping others. Without appropriate "self-care", I became drained and my mood started to go downward due to an inner bitterness between the unconscious and the conscious parts of my psyche. Some would say my soul became angry with me. It was great that I had been journaling. The pattern was obvious when I reviewed my journal with my trusted advisor. This made it easy to make some adjustments and become fulfilled again. From a fulfilled place of being, joy is easy.

It was not always this way. When I began this process, I did not have enough neural pathways which were capable of creating joy. I have spoken earlier about working on creating more positive thoughts, actions and feelings than negative each and every day. Journaling helped track this. When I had gotten to the point where my thoughts were increasingly more positive I continued to stop and reframe negative thoughts, actions and feelings to make them positive. It is a numbers game. I worked on literally creating a greater number of "joy" neurons than negative neurons through my daily "thought" practices and my actions.

Once I was doing that, it was important for me to continue to create joy. I have often struggled with being happy. I realized that behind everything I and many other people did and do was the desire to be happy. That is the main goal. I like to differentiate joy and happiness by saying that happiness is based on what happens around us that is why it is "happi" ness. Accordingly, I want to create joy just because I am breathing. That way, my happiness is not based on events (which have to be categorized as good or bad), except for the event of breathing. If breathing is not happening any more, then it will not matter if I am happy or not.

To get there I had to create the neural pathways. This requires feeling the joy physically. I learned that celebrating caused joyful feelings. So, I created the "Sweet Delicious Breath" exercise and then celebrated it. As I was shifting from being defined by what I had, owned or did as my job to being a human being worthy of joy just because I am breathing. I realized that I did not want things to make me happy.

As I said earlier, losing all of my worldly possessions and titles and the death of my identities which I had to endure was extremely painful. So, I decided to base my happiness and be grateful for something that could not be taken away and that I could keep with me. So, I chose my thumbnails. I decided that if I had my thumbnails, it would be a good day. Well, first of all, having thumbnails is not that enjoyable and second, someone pointed out to me that someone can take those away. So, I decided to base my joy on the fact that I was breathing.

I used to spend a significant amount of time snorkeling on the coast of Florida and in the Bahamas. I learned how to dive down 80 feet with a snorkel. Doing this requires holding my breath for two to four minutes. After I would dive down and hold my breath, when I would resurface, that first breath always tasted and felt amazing (I call this first breath the "Sweet Delicious Breath"). So, when I created the Sweet Delicious Breath exercise, I began by holding my breath and then feeling the first inhale. It feels good! I then would celebrate that with a celebratory motion of my arms, hands and body saying "Yes", "Yes", "Yes". This exercise hacks the hormones and nervous system to create a very joyful feeling. The body releases oxytocin, and other endorphins to make the body feel good. I would then celebrate that feeling and try to recreate it as much and for as long as possible.

Now consider that I suffer from chronic pain. As I mentioned earlier, I did so much damage to my body that I have had multiple surgeries including two hip replacements. Many people also suffer from chronic pain. Some say, "I don't want any pain!!" Issues with pain mean you have suffered in the past. People who have suffered without being able to find healing in the past may have a great aversion to any new possibilities of pain. The prospect of more pain brings up fear of getting even weaker.

Then there is the issue of vulnerability. All these issues run deep. They also all contribute to the level, strength and duration of pain. Often just worrying about pain can cause pain. I used to be extremely avoidant of the dentist. I did not want to go. I had experienced lots of pain at the dentist. In fact, to me it was basically an invitation for someone to hurt me. So, I avoided the dentist. Then one day my dentist said, "what are you so worried about." I said, "the pain you guys cause me." He said, "You are a grown man. Is it really that bad? Or do you think we are going to cause you some temporary or permanent damage?"

I decided to change my perspective. I realized that my anticipation of the pain was doing me more harm than the actual pain. I have endured lots of horrific pain in my life. So, what was I afraid of? It was just another unpleasant but necessary event. This greatly changed my experiences with going to the dentist. I was also able to apply this idea to all the pain in my life. I accept the pain as the price of my past.

My past has taught me how to live most of my days with a high level of bliss. I would rather be happy than sad and this is true regardless of pain. In other words, I would rather be in pain and happy than not in pain and miserable. After I made that decision and practiced it for 21 days, I soon found that all of my pain had lost a significant amount of power over how I felt and functioned. I also was in less pain. Was this my perspective or a physical truth? Frankly, I do not care because pain no longer affects my happiness. Acceptance has significant power! The work did and does not stop there. There are many other areas of the psyche to work on. This book will not cover all of the different areas that we work on daily. A few of them include full and complete self-acceptance, self-love, self-esteem, identity, purpose, self-actualization and humility.

Ideally, impatience also ends with acceptance. However, it is not that easy. As I stated earlier, I also released the idea that I knew how things were supposed to happen. The Homo sapiens nervous system is constantly trying to define our surroundings in order to keep us safe. I began to and continue to entrain my system that I want to live in an "undefined" world. My system still sends me messages about how things "should" be. I have to "DFM" those messages. I tell myself that my opinion of how things "should" be does not "F"ing matter. Full acceptance of all things does away with judgment, isolation, abandonment, the "need" for respect, frustration, anger and many more things. Mastering that is, in my experience, one of the most difficult and desired goals. It goes against our deepest instincts as Homo sapiens.

When you can go back inside yourself with enough acceptance and confidence to let awareness unfold, new understandings begin to become clear with the new awareness. Confidence cannot be forced. You will be adequate in your own eyes when you experience deeper and deeper levels of understanding. The journaling described above assists greatly in creating these new awarenesses and confidences. I remember sitting in courtrooms listening to the plaintiff's attorneys telling the judge what a bad person I was. It was hard to sit there in such a judgmental environment and listen to the negative attack on me. Since I had been journaling for years, I knew the truth. I was able to sit there and walk through all that ugliness by knowing that they had not nor would they ever read my journal and really get to know me.

If you are impatient, acceptance will help with that too. Avoiding anxiety and resolving inner conflict is an ongoing process of love and acceptance. This is not about flipping switches. We do not reach some place and get to stop striving for how we want to live life. As we progress, it gets easier. We reach plateaus of needing less inner work, just not "no" inner work.

We are planting seeds every day, nurturing the growth of those seedlings, continuing to grow; I believe growth is unlimited. The way you make seeds grow is with nourishment and for us nourishment comes from paying attention. Only a direct awareness with ourselves brings the nourishment of attention and the more nourishment we offer ourselves the greater our growth will be.

Over time and with appropriately applied NeuroEmpowerment, the feedback of EEG-neurofeedback, and Neurofeedforward, you will be able to see for yourself that your pain in your body is less and less and that your emotions have begun to change from despair (fear-based) to love and hope.

The by-product of this process is that the fear-based identity and resistance diminishes. Over time, it becomes easier and easier to say, "I can do this process, and I will." It is important to step by step, maintain your positive results. Our minds and our bodies begin working together, along with our new knowledge, training, and experience to form lasting results. This is how we get what we really, really want.

There is a "hero's journey" aspect to how our nervous system and neuroplasticity function. For many of us, love-based feelings are not ordinary. In the "hero's journey" they would be called extraordinary. For many of us, due to fear, it is "extraordinary" for us to just feel relaxed. In the "hero's journey" we have to venture into the extraordinary state of love-based functioning and practice (or journey into) creating love-based energy (thoughts, feelings, and actions) as much as possible until the extraordinary becomes ordinary. As we relax into our recovery from living from fear and into discovering what's possible from living from love, we relinquish our old beliefs about fear and self-worth.

What is even more powerful is that our past mistakes become important lessons we can gain from our past. They become stepping stones in our journey that are extremely valuable to fortify us to continue forward and live life differently than we have. This is often different than we are even familiar with. It may take us out of our comfort zone. Journaling and having a mentor or person we can speak to often regarding how we are doing is, again, a very valuable part of this process. We can journal and speak to our mentor about the questions of are we actually becoming a new person? The person we want to be? The best version of ourselves?

I have spoken much about fear. Fear is an illusion of the possibility of an event occurring in the future that relates to the past. I like to say that fear stands for

False Events Appearing Real

Fear is never real in the now. Fear is about an imagined event in the future that hasn't even happened yet. That means fear is about losing the fight with ourselves. Fear can be paralyzing and block our motivation to reach our goals. It is based on what we believe to be true about ourselves from past experiences. In other words, we can fear success or be consumed with worry or fear of failure, meaning we do believe we cannot have success at all. Often, it is worse than that. Often, we do not believe we are worthy of or deserve success. That's enough to make anyone anxious!

What We Do at The Supermind Center

As I said earlier, I made a decision to devote my life to helping people to go from not functioning well to functioning well. I have been doing that since 2001. I have discovered many things along the way. I wanted to be able to use the collective data from clients in order to help do my job better.

Unfortunately, without a substantial amount of funding it is almost impossible to get groups of people with the same issues in order to have a homogeneous sample pool of data I could work with. I realized that I could structure the work I was doing to develop a "homogeneous sample pool" (a group of study units that are alike enough to be studied as the same type of subjects).

I was looking at their neural activity, which means that what people thought about directly affected their brainwave graphs and the data. I realized that if I create a pre-planned set of sessions that directed the participants to think about the same thing in each session, I could use the brainwave data from each session as a homogeneous data pool to study.

I began creating standardized programs at the end of 2009. In this programming, everybody who came in had the same subject matter for the first 7 sessions. Specifically, each session has 7 to 12 mental exercises ranging from 5 to 20 minutes. For each exercise, the clients were directed what to think about and often what mantras to repeat during the exercise. Some of the exercises were done with their eyes closed, some were done open for the first half of the exercise and then closed for the second half, or they were done with their eyes open for the entire exercise. The direction for each exercise fits in the category of mindfulness, self-directed neuroplasticity, holistic (life and executive) coaching and cognitive behavior therapy (a form of psychology). Some people liken it to self-hypnosis or neural linguistic programming.

The sessions were planned out and adjusted based on how the people responded to each session. Due to the fact that many people were not thinking in patterns like the ones in the sessions, I realized that we were integrating psychological (mindfulness and coaching) techniques to help people develop new neural pathways that they did not have before. Since this form of therapy does not take clients "backwards" or "reset their brains", we created a new form of Neurofeedback that I call Neurofeedforward.

I have created at least 25 different "paths" and over 150 standardized sessions for different people to transition from who they are into the best version of themselves that they can be (according to them). After working with thousands of people over tens of thousands of sessions, we broke the code of what neurological patterns are required and are indicators for specific states of mind.

For example, if a person is too timid, we know the patterns of neural pathways to identify the accompanying belief systems which drive them to be timid. If they then want to be more outspoken, we can provide them with suggested belief systems for them to self-direct themselves to live by in order to activate the appropriate neural pathways which will help them become less timid.

At the same time, they would begin to do sessions with specific mantras which activate specific levels of their mind. During which we utilize the operant conditioning neurofeedback to allow them to train their nervous system to function more in line with how they desire. They are literally creating neural pathways which they did not have before in our Neurofeedforward programming.

We create options for dealing with different levels of the psyche and how to function fearlessly. While fear patterns reduce in the nervous system, we help create love-based neural pathways anchored in knowing that it is ok to be safe. In this way, participants move from being fear-based to being love-based.

At The Supermind Center we are committed to helping people recondition and influence their nervous systems to function more the way they want including recovery from bodily pain and mental pain. Here are some examples of mantras used in the session to reach client goals.

- I want to know that I am safe.
- I want to be pain free in order to resume my desired activities.
- I want to follow my dream and my goal of creating my heart's desires (such as better relationships).
- I want to be able to accept my mistakes and myself as a person.
- I want to free myself from anxiety.
- I want to free myself from depression.
- I want to free myself from fear.
- I want to love myself and others.
- I want to feel self-confident and all the energy I need in order to have the success I desire.
- I want to live life from a place of love rather than fear.

Without the brain-computer interface of the neurotechnology utilized as we use it, these types of mantras or changes can take many days (months or even years) of asking the same question or stating the same mantra over and over. It also may take separate time periods of work for the many different areas of our lives such as family, career, friendship, self-identity and the physical body. It may also not even be possible. Some patterns are ingrained so deeply that without the technology, we cannot break those patterns or build enough alternative patterns to be able make the change.

Another powerful tool we guide people to use is "imagination". Imagine or visualize yourself restored, refreshed and existing as you want to be already. Imagine as clearly as you can just how that would feel in every situation. If you spend a few minutes each day imagining living the way you want to be and having all that you want, you are creating new neural pathways and a new relationship with yourself through your visualization. This will take some time. It is an inside job. It helps to coordinate the inside job with outside behaviors and environment.

Sitting in silence is a good way to become aware of "where you are". Are you feeling carefree today, happy, grateful etc.? Once you become more and more aware of how you are feeling and functioning, you can then begin to move in the direction you want to go! This also helps you to develop "discernment". Your awareness can function as a chain reaction. The flow of this chain reaction can take many forms. Most people have a level of consciousness that is resistant to the chain reaction. Your awareness is strengthened through practice. So, it is important to spend a few minutes each day paying attention to yourself, how you feel and how you want to feel.

Your vision is at first only a thought and of no value until it has been transformed into the mental state or behavior you desire. Should you slip back into old habits you can get right back on track by going back over and over to your imagined self. Your cause can be put back in motion. You (the conscious you) can be the driver of your own motivational bus. Your physical body is trained by your genetics, perceptions and life. It can want to begin to move into the state of taking action. You can trigger your own possibilities! You can propel yourself into taking action. You can make a decision to be and get what you want (you may have to make the decision daily for a while). That's it! Do this every day for fifteen minutes. This is a gateway into a better life (because your perception of your life can get better).

You can begin by dedicating 15 minutes to be with yourself (if that seems too long, start at 5 minutes) without fear and worry. For so many years you probably have had some angst about going back out into the world, and to your workplace and even your family as the new you. Sometimes just thinking about being out in the world can cause anxiety and depression.

Those memories come up, even though you don't want them to because they have been programmed in your brain and body, by your genetics, perceptions and past experiences. This practice will teach you how to un-program all the old mistakes and begin to show you that you are becoming more aware of who you are now and feeling good about your changes. You cannot force or push out the past, but you can relieve yourself from the anxiety of the past through some simple steps to be practiced every day at the time you choose is best for you.

We have to fully process and reconcile our past for it to stop affecting our emotional sobriety. The way to process and reconcile our past is to accept that it happened (it is as it is - rather than try to understand why) and forgive all those involved, including the world, society, institutions, the government, people, and most importantly ourselves. This also may require forgiving that it happened even though it is "wrong" or "does not make sense". Sometimes we have to just decide that we would rather be happy than "right". It is important to do this over and over again until our past no longer affects how we feel today and the embedded triggers lose their power.

There is only one way to make this happen. Begin. After ten or twelve times of practicing, you may start to "get it" that you are no longer the same as you were before. You can feel just plain good knowing that, and that can help you to continue to practice. This will make more sense to you as you persist. It feels good to drive your motivational bus. Unfortunately, based on how deeply the neural pathways containing the old "you" that you want to change are ingrained inside of you, you may not be able to do this on your own without the help that we give at The Supermind Center or through some other similar modality.

Look for support that will help you be the best version of yourself (according to you), not just try to make you "normal". This process requires a conscious awareness and ability to change beliefs and the making of coordinated changes with the subconscious and unconscious. The person helping you to make these kinds of changes has to understand and be able to work with these variables in order to be effective and keep you safe. This is what we excel at The Supermind Center.

Key Takeaways

Resistance to Change:
- Involuntary nervous system prioritizes survival, causing resistance.
- Lack of neural pathways for change may be accelerated through feedback systems.

Overcoming Overwhelm and Fear:
- Stress and overwhelm from clinging to old beliefs lead to fear-driven responses.
- NeuroEmpowerment, especially Neurofeedforward, creates new pathways for lasting transformation.

Self-Reflection for Clarity:
- Regular self-reflection clarifies desires, fostering personal growth.
- Patience in waiting for clear answers enhances understanding.

Pursuit of Happiness:
- Acknowledge happiness as a goal, addressing resistance rooted in past experiences.
- Embrace transformation and self-understanding using the power of imagination.

Overcoming Limits and Safety Transformation:
- Challenge limiting beliefs and shift from fear-driven instincts to love-driven living.
- Use a formulated approach to address deep-seated notions of safety.

Empowering Personal Responsibility:
- Challenge justifications, emphasizing personal agency.
- Encourage self-reflection without shame, fostering responsibility for change.

Transformative Power of Connection:
- Illustrate change through vulnerability, self-awareness, and connection.
- Shift from fear-based mentalities to self-love for personal and communal growth.

Neurological Transformation and Belief Systems:
- Highlight interplay between psychological and physiological changes
- Emphasize intentional retraining to override instinctual responses.

Key Takeaways

Societal Power Dynamics:
- Critique societal suppression of individual power in favor of conformity.
- Advocate for internal development and self-reliance over external solutions.

Dependency on External Solutions:
- Expose reliance on pills, emphasizing the need for internal development.
- Shift towards developing coping skills rather than depending on external interventions.

Evolution Beyond Tribal Dependence:
- Advocate for individual and communal focus on personal growth.
- Free from conforming to communal identities in the era beyond tribal survival.

Empowering Inner Peace:
- Stress the challenge of finding inner peace amidst natural instincts.
- Emphasize transformative power of creating inner peace for enhanced strength.

Meditation and Self-Betterment:
- Use meditation gradually and introduce Self-Betterment Exercises.
- Acknowledge struggles and ongoing progress in the pursuit of self-betterment.

Acceptance and Growth:
- Advocate for acceptance, addressing impatience in the self-improvement process.
- Highlight continuous growth through journaling, self-discovery, and overcoming fear-based illusions.

Supermind Mission and Background:
- Recognized the need for homogeneous data, leading to structured programs for collective study.
- Neurofeedforward Programming: Developed standardized programs for self-improvement. Used Neurofeedforward to reshape neural pathways for fear to love-based functioning.

THE NEUROEMPOWERMENT PROCESS

I am going to review some tools and techniques that we teach in the NeuroEmpowerment process. This begins with learning how to cope with how we feel. Based on my experience, applying the suggestions in this book could work (provide some measure of relief from anxiety, improve mood, or improve sleep) for approximately 75% of the people who read this book. For further help, it makes sense to find help like what we provide through NeuroEmpowerment at The Supermind Center.

Since many of the feelings we have are not truly based on what is happening right where we are at that moment, we begin with getting into the now. One of the easiest ways to tap into the now and be present (at whatever level) is to focus on our breathing. My suggestion is to breathe in for the count of three, hold the breath for three and then breathe out for three. Do that for three sets and be thankful for how good that breath feels. If you are safe and have nothing to worry about (because you get to choose!), then celebrate that!

. Just breathe, celebrate and enjoy that. This will help calm the nervous system down. Enjoy how nice that feels.

This may be difficult when you first try it. More practice makes it easier. More practice also allows us to do it longer and have more profound experiences of self-awareness and peace. As time goes on and we do this day after day, our nervous system will be more conditioned to function this way automatically, which will bring more calmness and peace into our days without having to think about it.

The next thing we want to work on is learning how to elevate our mood. This is not a common theme in our society. Celebrate the small stuff. Celebrate your new awareness. Celebrate what you can achieve. Celebrate gaining control of your nervous system.

These tools have helped many people find more peace. However, I like to take the "coping" with life tools a step further. Now it is time to change our perspective of what to cope with. Remember that our animal instincts (aka tribal instincts, survival instincts, herd instincts) are fear based. They drive us to feel that we are rarely safe and if we get safe we put up walls and get weapons in order to stay safe (slight exaggeration). So, the next item to work on is fear itself. As stated by President Franklin D. Roosevelt, "There is nothing to fear but fear itself."

Become Aware

Unfortunately, fear is pervasive and affects us in many different ways at many different levels of our existence. Fear is such a part of our lives that many of us have no idea that we are acting in fear. In my experience, 95% of people are acting from fear more than 90% of the time. It is very difficult to see at first. Awareness is important, so that is a good place to start.

Let's start with becoming aware of the "need" to define ourselves and our surroundings. This is a constant part of our daily lives. It is entirely based on fear. A place to begin is to utilize the mantra "I want to live from a place of love rather than fear" as often as possible and in as many situations or decisions as possible. To also really make this work it is important to decide to behave in accordance with love. I keep the "love" passage from the Bible, which is read at so many weddings on my phone. This passage reads,

> *If I have a faith that can move mountains, but do not have love, I am nothing. If I give all I possess to the poor and give over my body to hardship that I may boast, but do not have love, I gain nothing. Love is patient, love is kind. It does not envy, it does not boast, it is not proud. It does not dishonor others, it is not self-seeking, it is not easily angered, it keeps no record of wrongs. Love does not delight in evil but rejoices with the truth. It always protects, always trusts, always hopes, always perseveres. Love never fails. But where there are prophecies, they will cease; where there are tongues, they will be stilled; where there is knowledge, it will pass away. For we know in part and we prophesy in part, but when completeness comes, what is in part disappears. When I was a child, I talked like a child, I thought like a child, I reasoned like a child. When I became a man, I put the ways of childhood behind me. For now, we see only a reflection as in a mirror; then we shall see face to face. Now I know in part; then I shall know fully, even as I am fully known. And now these three remain: faith, hope and love. But the greatest of these is love.*[18]

I spent some time reading this at least once per day. Upon deep reflection, this provides a great guide as to the characteristics and mindset of a person who comes from love. There is also a prayer that I alter for non-believers. Prayer is a great self-motivational device. Just take out the word "Lord". This prayer is known as the prayer of St. Francis and provides a great behavioral guide for behaving from "love."

Prayer of St. Francis
(excerpt)

Lord, make me an instrument of your peace.
Where there is hatred, let me bring love.
Where there is offense, let me bring pardon.
Where there is discord, let me bring union.
Where there is error, let me bring truth.
Where there is doubt, let me bring faith.
Where there is despair, let me bring hope.
Where there is darkness, let me bring your light.
Where there is sadness, let me bring joy.
O Master, let me not seek as much
to be consoled as to console,
to be understood as to understand,
to be loved as to love,
for it is in giving that one receives,
it is in self-forgetting that one finds,
it is in pardoning that one is pardoned,

Forget that this is a prayer. It is a great guide on how to live from love rather than fear in many areas of life.

Fear blocks us from acting in the above-mentioned ways. Now with our new awareness, we can face those fears, take a real look at them, and realize we are ready, willing, and able to change and get rid of those old fears and old beliefs. This is another time to apply the "first thought wrong" way of living I discussed earlier.

Fear-based functioning is a natural part of being human. Our nervous systems naturally contain a focus to help us survive. When we are making this transition from being fear-based to being love based it is necessary to understand that our bodies take longer to change and adapt than our minds. Our senses (eyes, ears, nose etc.) inherently provide us information from a fear perspective. It will take time and determination to be able to entrain that signaling to take place from love rather than fear. It is important for us to practice love-based feelings steadily and consistently in order to get our unconscious (inter-cellular) functioning to make the transition fully.

We want to allow the first "thought" or signal coming from our subconscious to come into our awareness without reaction in order to review the information provided with the "first thought wrong" understanding. We then want to reformat our perspective from love and then direct our subconscious that these types of thoughts no longer serve us and from now on to provide signals from "love".

Following this procedure over and over again will stop the "circular thinking" described earlier. If we are intentional and diligent about following this process, sooner or later it will become natural for our senses to start signaling from love in lieu of fear. Over time, the "first thought" will begin to become "right" and we will not have to follow the process anymore.

Live Courageously

Just remember: courage is as contagious as fear. When we act from love, we are acting with courage. Courage is the measure of our heartfelt participation in life, with one-another, with work, community, and a brighter future. To be courageous is not necessarily to go anywhere or do anything except to be aware of those things we already feel deeply, and then to live through the unending vulnerabilities of those consequences.

Courage is what love looks like when tested by the necessities of being alive. Only by looking back does it look like courage. The testing ground for courage, as it is for love, is often a crisis, those trying and troubled times where our hearts must go to work, and during which our true strength of character is revealed.

One of the most prominent testing grounds is relationships. Relationships often force us to be courageous with our feelings deep in the body and in the world. When we can be true to ourselves as a part of loving ourselves, it becomes easier to live up to and into the necessities of relationships, even those that often already exist. The true self, nurtured and developed through self-love, pushes us forward to help us be the best version of ourselves. Be courageous! Enjoy the fruits that love brings.

"Crisis is unavoidable."[19] Every human life seems to be drawn eventually, as if by some unspoken parallel, some tidal flow or underground magnetic field, toward the raw dynamic essentials of its existence, as if everything up to that point had been a preparation for a meeting, for a confrontation in an elemental form with our essential flaws, and with what an individual could only receive stepped down, interpreted or diluted.

Crisis includes what has been described as "the dark night of the soul". It is like two immense storm fronts fighting for their existence within us. The storm front of what overwhelms human beings from the inside (our inner demons) and the storm front of what overpowers us from the outside. Holding them together is the hardest place to stay. It is better to make a world of both and to be active in their exchange, aware of our need to be needed, our wish to be seen, able to be found by the living world and have the ability to forget self and respond to its call when needed. Through love, we can weather and learn from the storms, dark nights of the soul, or fear.

Courage is a mechanism of our nervous system which allows us to act in accordance with the characteristics of love even when we are afraid. Through this and faith we can "fake it until we make it", so to speak. By doing this, we are building the neural pathways which contain the functioning required to live from love rather than fear.

Love is a trinity. Love is a feeling or emotion, Love is an action, and love is receiving. We cannot love others without loving ourselves. When looking at our daily lives when we are deciding how to feel, behave and function, it is helpful to look at everything in our lives and think about why it is important. Is it aligned with your values (loving yourself), or is it something you are considering due to fear? Tough question sometimes.

What Are Your Values Exercise

What are our values? Get a pencil and paper (or use whatever you use in today's world to make notes) or just write in this book. Identify the values which apply. Before doing this exercise, try to decide which values you "like" without tribal instincts being your guide. Tribal instincts will say to you, I "need" this value because I cannot provide it for myself. So consider, do I want to interact with a person or set of persons on a daily basis if they do not share this value with me.

Value list (a good list - not necessarily all inclusive - please feel free to add)

Adventure	Excitement
Affiliation	Family
Accountability	Friendship
Acceptance	Free Time For You
Achievement	Freedom
Adaptability	Fun
Ambition	Gratitude
Appreciation	Growth
Attraction	Honesty
Authenticity	Integrity
Balance	Loyalty
Beauty	Love
Celebration	Powerful
Challenge	Precision
Creativity	Prestige
Communication	Relaxation
Commitment	Respect
Compassion	Safety
Confidence	Security
Courage	Spiritual Unity
Curiosity	Support
Enjoyment of living	Validation
Equality	Worthiness

Look over this list carefully and consider which of these are important to you. Then take a moment to rank them in order of importance from 1 being the most important to 10 (or 1 to 46) being the least.

The next question is - do you treat yourself or give these values to yourself (as is possible) or do you look to get them from others?

The next question is - do you believe you are worthy and deserve the values you find important?

If after you have made the list, you answer one or both of the previous questions with a "no" or a "not exactly", then there is work to be done. Take the list with you, contemplate the list, and incorporate knowing you are worthy and treating yourself in accordance with the appropriate values.

After you have made the list and answered the two previous questions with a resounding yes, then go back to the list. Now let's review the list in another way. Think of each person in your life and what value do they help you with or treat you with. If you are treating yourself with value and know you are worthy, then aligning with the people, places, and things that treat you in line with your values becomes less of a "need" and more of a "want."

We may find that we have some people, places, and things in our lives out of convenience or fear. At the very least, this exercise will assist us in having more mature and loving relationships.

These values represent the states you can move toward to be happy and satisfied with yourself. They are states you want to experience or avoid. When your important needs are gratified more by you than others you can be more comfortable while obtaining and being who you really are. You can feel more passionate and ready to find your real purpose. In other words, when you experience what is important to you, your energy gets kicked off.

When you know what is important to you, you will feel a spark produced by your new energy. At that point, there is no going back to depression, anxiety, and fear. All of those old states are replaced with the energy to move forward step by step and enjoy each day on your path. Down days may come and go, but by following this path we can overcome those negative energies (sadness, anger, or depression). They will lose their strength, come less often and last less time. Trying to reflect on this and enjoying the journey is extremely helpful.

Tell someone you trust or who wants to help you know what is important to you. It will feel good just to talk about it. When you are in this process of finding out what is important to you, ask your heart, not your head what is really important.

One example is the importance of being creative: A friend found herself in a wheelchair after a car accident and was confined to it for a year. She had just learned how to play the guitar while taking lessons with her 12-year-old son. One day she had a really creative idea. She called the guitar teacher and made a proposal. She asked the teacher if she could teach the beginning guitar course right from her wheelchair. The community center was two blocks away and her son could wheel her there and assist passing out the guitars that were provided. The teacher said, "Yes!" She had been sitting in the wheelchair depressed at her situation, and her courage to be that creative led her on her path to recovery.

If creativity is important to you, you can ask yourself, "What have I been creative about in the past?" If security is important to you, you may ask yourself, "How can I achieve being more secure?" Each question you ask of yourself will bring an answer. If you remain unsure, ask five trusted friends or people. See which answers feel good deep down.

Often, you will be aware of what steps to take immediately and that will give you a good feeling right away. If the steps do not become obvious, it does not hurt to ask your five people for help and again see what resonates (feels good to you).

If the old fears turn up once again, you can "first thought wrong" them and find the courage to take one step, and then another, and remember each step is taking you to exactly what is important to you. When you move toward your values, those which are important, you become fulfilled.

It boils down to changing your thinking because you are heavily affected by what you think about! And what you think about expands. Oops, that means if you are thinking about how afraid you are, you will become more afraid. That's for sure not what you want. So, once again, ask yourself, "What do I really, really want?" Review your values list again. make adjustments as necessary.

What you really want will come back into your mind. You return to thinking about what you want and then allow your imagination and your dream or visualization to come back into your mind, as if you already are what you so deeply desire. The old thoughts driven by fear, anxiety, depression or doubt may occasionally come back. That is ok, just dismiss them again. The best news of all is that when your new thinking of possibility within yourself becomes stronger and stronger, the fear can fade away permanently. And it will!

Fear actually becomes less prevalent! New beliefs will be cast in your mind. "I can do this, and I will! Step by step, I am learning and restoring myself" And then, you will begin to believe it. That's the best feeling! Celebrate it. Say "Yes! Yes! Yes!" while throwing your arms up in the air and it will get anchored more deeply in your body.

Remember, this is a process. All of our experiences affect and influence our nervous systems and all levels of our mind and body to varying degrees. What we have laid down inside of us in the past will remain for quite a while. The deeper down in our consciousness these parts of us are, the less control we have over them (both in the process of living and in living in the now). But our intentions for each part of us give us the ability to influence how they function.

There may be some "push me - pull me" or up and down sensations as we build new patterns and work to stop using the old ones. What is important to note is that we can become aware of the patterns in our mind and body which frees us from being enslaved by them and allows us to have intentional input as to how they function. We can change their effect upon us by changing our thought processes and behaviors.

Most of what I have been talking about in this book is working on our inner world contained in our nervous systems. The outer world is a reflection of the collective inner worlds of all of us. So, as it goes inside of us all is how it goes collectively for us all.

Everything begins inside you. If the engine of your car is not working, you don't go out and polish the car, right? Rather you check the inner workings, the source of what makes your automobile run. In this regard, you also go to your own source or your inner thoughts. For example, think a thought, reap an emotion. "How do I want to feel," you ask yourself. What determines our feelings or our emotions? What we focus on, correct? It is a little bit more complicated than that.

Our unconscious is affected by many variables in our past which affect how we function now. Our subconscious drives how we process and is strongly affected by how the unconscious is functioning (based heavily on the past) and how the conscious levels are functioning also (based in the now). Our conscious mind manages our thoughts in the now which are driven by our beliefs first and then the subconscious and unconscious levels of the psyche. We want to make the decisions that lead to our feeling good in every area of our lives, minds, and bodies.

Here is a secret; hold your intentions as if you are already on the road to achieving them. Emotion is created by energy in motion. The opposite can also be true. If you focus on fear, you feel more fear. When you feel fear, you are firing up and strengthening the "fear" neurons and neural pathways. It is physically true that what you focus on grows. It makes sense, right? So, focus on what you really want and observe yourself. Yes, become the observer that you are creating what you really want. That in itself, at the very least, creates the positive energy to take action towards your goals.

Remember, you are the creator and the observer. Most of the time the "you" creator is involuntary. That involuntary part of you can be programmed to change. That is what this book has all been about! Take responsibility for programming your own subconscious and unconscious functions and soon you will be living a "fantastic!" life anxiety free.

Relax, feel at peace and do not feel that this change is too hard to accomplish. Realize you're on your way to becoming that person you really want to be. Feel the confidence invading your mind and your psyche knowing that this is a part of your journey. Enjoy the process as well as the outcomes.

In closing, I want to thank you for reading this book. I intend to help as many people as I can to stop living in fear and live from love. I humbly hope that you may be one of those people as soon as possible. Woohoo! Enjoy!

Key Takeaways

Present Moment Awareness:
- Begin with focused breathing to tap into the present moment, calming the nervous system and enhancing self-awareness.

Elevate Mood and Celebrate:
- Shift societal norms by celebrating small achievements and fostering a positive outlook, gaining control of the nervous system.

Addressing Fear-Based Functioning:
- Recognize and confront pervasive fear, employing mantras and behavioral changes to shift from fear to love-based living.

Values Exercise Takeaways:

Identifying Core Values:
- Reflect on personal values, prioritizing them without succumbing to tribal instincts. Recognize values that align with genuine preferences.

Self-Treatment vs. External Validation:
- Evaluate whether personal values are fulfilled through self-treatment or external validation. Recognize the importance of self-worth in the pursuit of values.

Aligning with Relationships:
- Assess relationships based on their alignment with personal values. Shift from "need" to "want" in relationships, fostering mature and loving connections.

ENDNOTES

1. National Center for Mind-Body Medicine. (2000). Retrieved from https://www.netmindbody.com/

2. National Institutes of Health. (2001). Neuroscience (2nd ed.). Neural Circuits. Retrieved from https://www.ncbi.nlm.nih.gov/books/NBK11154/

3. National Institutes of Health. (2023). Brain Basics: The Life and Death of a Neuron. Retrieved from https://www.ninds.nih.gov/health-information/public-education/brain-basics/brain-basics-life-and-death-neuron#:~:text=Neurons%20are%20information%20messengers.,cord%2C%20and%20the%20entire%20body.

4. Boldrini, M., Fulmore, C. A., Tartt, A. N., Simeon, L. R., Pavlova, I., Poposka, V., ... Mann, J. J. (5 April 2018). Human hippocampal neurogenesis persists throughout aging. Cell Stem Cell, 22(4), 589–599.e5. https://doi.org/10.1016/j.stem.2018.03.015

5. Cleveland Clinic. (2023, March 3.). Fetal Development: Stages of Growth. Retrieved from https://my.clevelandclinic.org/health/articles/7247-fetal-development-stages-of-growth

6. Boss, M. (1965). A Psychiatrist Discovers India. Oswald Wolff.

7. Psychology Today. (n.d.). Emotional Intelligence. Retrieved from https://www.psychologytoday.com/us/basics/emotional-intelligence

8. Psychology Tools. (n.d.). Fight or Flight Response. Retrieved from https://www.psychologytools.com/resource/fight-or-flight-response/

9. Cohut, M. (2018, April 10). What to know about the fight or flight response. Medical News Today. Retrieved from https://www.medicalnewstoday.com/articles/320172

10. National Heart, Lung, and Blood Institute. (n.d.). Education and Awareness: Sleep Health. Retrieved from https://www.nhlbi.nih.gov/health-topics/education-and-awareness/sleep-health

11. Psychology Today. (2022, September 15). Biofeedback. Retrieved from https://www.psychologytoday.com/us/therapy-types/biofeedback

12. Psychology Today. (n.d.). Behaviorism. Retrieved from https://www.psychologytoday.com/us/basics/behaviorism

13. Amstadter, A. B. (2008). Emotion Regulation and Anxiety Disorders. Journal of Anxiety Disorders, 22(2), 211–221. https://doi.org/10.1016/j.janxdis.2007.02.004. PMCID: PMC2736046. PMID: 17349775.

14. Tan, S. Y., & Yip, A. (2018). Hans Selye (1907–1982): Founder of the stress theory. Singapore Medical Journal, 59(4), 170–171. https://doi.org/10.11622/smedj.2018043. PMCID: PMC5915631. PMID: 29748693.

15. Brown, B. B. (1977). Stress and the Art of Biofeedback. Oswald Wolff.

16. Yucha, C. B., Clark, L., Smith, M., Uris, P., LaFleur, B., & Duval, S. (2001). The effect of biofeedback in hypertension. Applied Nursing Research, 14(1), 29–35. https://doi.org/10.1053/apnr.2001.21078

17. Shimizu, K., Inage, K., Morita, M. et al. New treatment strategy for chronic low back pain with alpha wave neurofeedback. Sci Rep 12, 14532 (2022). https://doi.org/10.1038/s41598-022-18931-0

18. The Bible. 1 Corinthians 13. In New International Version. Retrieved from https://www.biblegateway.com/passage/?search=1%20Corinthians%2013&version=NIV#fen-NIV-28669b

19. Whyte, D. (2015, March 27). CRISIS is unavoidable. Every human life seems to be drawn eventually, as if by some unspoken parallel, some tidal flow... [Facebook post]. Facebook. https://www.facebook.com/PoetDavidWhyte/photos/crisisis-unavoidable-every-human-life-seems-to-be-drawn-eventually-as-if-by-some/1124387200920615/?paipv=0&eav=Afb9wlORKA7j22ZEzjkwwgPiEmtZmqzfueWvDlqzE5vmnITz2PA7WWeRXTB5uBIWlvk&_rdr

Forthcoming by Geoffrey Cole with Bootstrap Publications

21-Day Guide to Anxiety Free Living
How to Live Anxiety Free Journal
New Bad Word Books for Babies
The Subtle Art of DFM
Proverbs for Dinner

Thank you for reading How to Live Anxiety Free. To continue exploring the themes discussed in this book, access additional resources, or to connect with the community, visit www.howtoliveanxietyfree.com
Instagram: @realgcole

www.ingramcontent.com/pod-product-compliance
Lightning Source LLC
Chambersburg PA
CBHW071357120626
46546CB00002B/729